Great Welsh
WALKS

Acknowledgements

I love walking in Wales and feel very lucky to have been given the opportunity to make a TV series and write a book about it. However, I could not have done either without the help of so many kind and wonderful people.

Firstly, a big thanks to all the guides for sharing their knowledge and enthusiasm for their corner of the country; to Gareth Rhys Rowlands my director/ producer for his wisdom and guidance and for being a top bloke; and Christina Macaulay, my executive producer, for all her hard work in making *Weatherman Walking* such a success.

To Martin Aaron for co-writing this book and for his photography skills; the skilled camera and sound crew; the production team for their patience and dedication; to Adrian Davies for supporting the series over the years. To my colleagues on the weather team for standing in for me so I could film the series; to Robat Gruffudd and the rest of the publishing team at Y Lolfa in Ceredigion; also to the Met Office for their support – and a big thank you to Penny Arnold who first came up with the idea of a series called *Weatherman Walking*.

To everyone else at BBC Cymru Wales for their assistance – I am privileged to work with so many talented people. And last, but by no means least, a huge thanks to you for watching the show and for reading this book. Keep smiling and happy walking!

DEREK BROCKWAY

Great Welsh
WALKS

Derek Brockway
and Martin Aaron

BBC | cymru wales

y Lolfa

First impression: 2014
© BBC Cymru Wales and Y Lolfa Cyf., 2014

The publishers wish to acknowledge the support of
Cyngor Llyfrau Cymru.

Photographs by Martin Aaron
Text by Derek Brockway and Martin Aaron
Book design by Robat Gruffudd / Y Lolfa

ISBN: 978-1-84771-821-1

Printed, published and bound in Wales
by Y Lolfa Cyf., Talybont, Ceredigion SY24 5HE
e-mail ylolfa@ylolfa.com
website www.ylolfa.com
tel. 01970 832 304
fax 832 782

Put your boots on!

Being a BBC weatherman is my dream job. Work has taken me around the UK and abroad – even as far as the Falkland Islands! But Wales will always be home and, in my opinion, there's no better place to live, or to go walking.

We've been filming *Weatherman Walking* since 2006. Over the space of seven series we've covered around 60 walks all over Wales, yet there's always something new to be discovered.

We're so lucky to have so much variety packed into one small country. From the steep hills and mountains of Snowdonia to the flat Millennium Coastal Park along the Loughor Estuary, from the ups and downs of the Pembrokeshire Coast Path to zigzagging along the Offa's Dyke Path – Wales is made for walking.

There are 18 walks in this book, suitable for all abilities, and though it only scratches the surface, it gives you a good taste of what our country has to offer.

Walking is fun, free, helps keep you fit, and is a great way to discover Wales. Whatever the weather, there's so much to see and do with a treasure trove of walks, and some of the best scenery in the world right on your doorstep.

It really is worth getting out there, and enjoying what wonderful Wales has to offer, even in the rain. So what are you waiting for? Put your boots on, grab your waterproofs, and don't forget to check the forecast before you go.

Derek Brockway

Introduction

Growing up in Pembroke-shire, I've been spoilt by breathtaking views from an early age – being dragged along on coastal forays by my parents and taking the magical landscape a little bit for granted.

It's only when you leave Wales that you realise just how special it is and there aren't many places that can compare with our country for its sheer rugged beauty.

I've always loved wildlife and the great outdoors – fishing, swimming, diving and surfing, a pastime that over the last 25 years has prevented me from venturing too far inland!

I began working on the website for *Weatherman Walking* back in 2001, firstly on the original Radio Wales programmes and then creating content to accompany the popular TV series.

I donned my official pair of BBC walking boots in 2009, left my keyboard behind and finally got to accompany Derek and a talented crew on the walks – taking photographs, mapping and writing up the routes for the viewers at home to enjoy. It's been a great experience, hard work and long days filming but we've had a great time along the way and met some fantastic guides.

I now have a long list of places that I'd probably never have visited if left to my own devices. I'm always biased towards the coastal walks but some of my personal inland favourites include:

Abergynolwyn *in the foothills of Snowdonia, for its waterfalls and views from the crumbling battlements of Castell y Bere in the late afternoon sunlight.*

Llanberis *for the sheer size and drama of the surrounding slate quarries and the panoramic views over Snowdon and the surrounding peaks.*

Penmaenmawr *for the expansive views, ancient stones and the magical descent into Rowen village via an old Roman track.*

We've literally travelled the length and breadth of the country to walk in some of the most dramatic locations Wales has to offer, which you'll hopefully be inspired to visit, now you've picked up this book.

Enjoy!

Martin Aaron

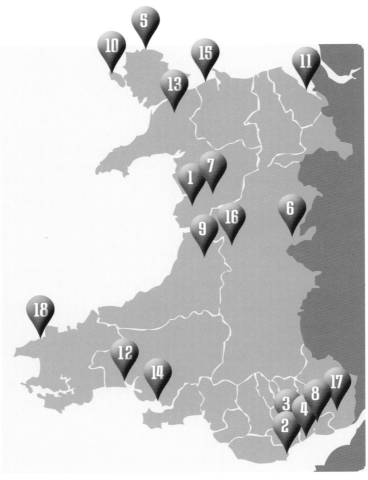

Please note that the maps included in this book are intended as a guide only. We have included OS coordinates to help you along the way, but the BBC and Y Lolfa cannot be held responsible for any accident or injury that may occur while following the routes. Routes and conditions may also have changed since publication. Always wear appropriate clothing and footwear and check weather conditions before heading out.

The Walks

Derek says. . .

STEAM TRAINS, a magnificent hilltop castle surrounded by mountains and converging rivers make this a walk to remember in the Snowdonia National Park.

The thing I like most about this walk is that it is so varied with history and wonderful views too.

I really enjoyed looking around the ruins of Castell y Bere which are in a spectacular location in the shadow of Cader Idris. Entry is free and it is well worth a visit if only for the fantastic views of the Dysynni valley towards Craig yr Aderyn (Bird Rock).

At Llanfihangel-y-Pennant, make sure you pop into St Michael's Church. This lovely old church had an important part to play in Welsh history given its association with Mary Jones. In 1800, she walked barefoot to Bala, 26 miles away, to buy a copy of the Welsh Bible.

In Abergynolwyn, there is a great café inside the community centre where we stopped for lunch, or if you fancy a shandy, the Railway Arms is just across the road.

The Talyllyn Railway is close by too and travels from Tywyn to Abergynolwyn and onto Nant Gwernol, which is where we start our walk in this beautiful part of Wales.

1. Abergynolwyn

Approximate distance: 6 miles

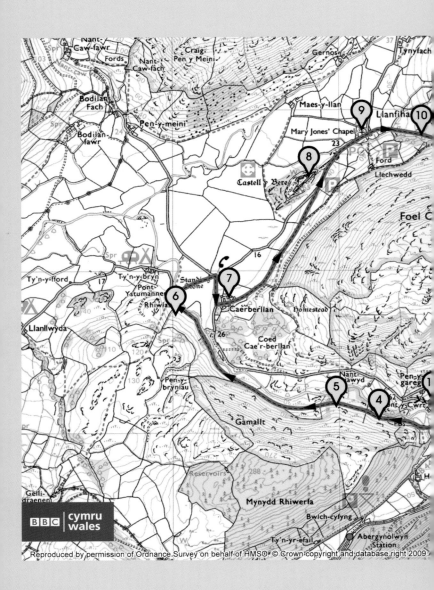

Abergynolwyn

Start / End

0.62 miles

Great Welsh Walks

Distance: *6 miles*
Map: *OS Explorer Map OL23*
Introduction: *A 6 mile circular walk through the foothills of Cader Idris in the Snowdonia National Park. Starting at the railway station of Nant Gwernol, you'll pass through the former slate mining village of Abergynolwyn on your way towards the ruins of Castell y Bere, a castle perched high on a rocky crag. From there you'll follow the road to Mary Jones's Chapel and through rolling hills and hidden valleys with ancient oaks and fast-flowing streams before dropping back down into the village.*

1. Start of the walk – Nant Gwernol railway station: SH 681066

The walk begins at Nant Gwernol railway station near Abergynolwyn where steam trains used to transport slate from the nearby Bryn Eglwys Quarry to the rest of the country.

The railway was an important part of the community here, linking the village via Tywyn with Birmingham and London, and providing a vital supply line. In the 1920s, families could hire a slate truck for the day to ride around in, as a summer treat.

The station is now served by a small passenger steam train carrying people between Nant Gwernol and Tywyn on the coast. It's situated in a spectacular spot, above a wooded valley with streams and waterfalls.

From the station platform follow a narrow, muddy track towards Nant Gwernol footbridge spanning the river below.

There's a track leading up the hill but don't take that one, stay on the signposted 'green route'.

From the bridge you'll have an amazing view of a waterfall cascading down the hillside and a nice view of the route through the valley ahead. Take care crossing the bridge as it can get fairly slippery underfoot, as Derek found out!

Turn left at the end of the bridge and keep walking down through the valley. There are steps leading up a track here but this is marked as an orange or blue route, so ignore these and keep walking.

The track can be muddy and uneven in places, so watch your footing. But don't forget to look around you and enjoy the waterfalls and clear pools as you go.

There's a wide variety of bird life in the valley – from dippers and grey wagtails in the streams, to the goldcrests, coal tits, redpolls and crossbills in the trees above.

2. Former quarrymen's houses: SH 678070

Near the top of the track you'll pass a stone bench and a Woodland Trust sign marked 'Coed Nant Gwernol'. Head down the hill along a tarmac road into the village, passing old quarrymen's houses on your right.

These attractive stone-block terraces were built to last and have lovely views over the hillsides. Opposite the cottages is the village Post Office with a fabulous café if you're hungry, and a curious wooden sculpture outside.

The sculpture features two river nymphs which, according to legend, represent the rivers Gwernol and Dysynni which meet in the village.

Cross over the main road following signs for the castle and walk down Llanegryn Street, where you'll pass more quarrymen's cottages.

3. Capel y Cwrt: SH 676071

At the end of the road before the stone bridge is an area known as Cwrt, which is the original name of the village when it was a small hamlet.

Turn left at the chapel and walk down behind the quarrymen's houses and along Water Street. Turn right onto a rusty metal footbridge and cross over the river.

Once across, follow a path through a marshy field near to where the two rivers, Gwernol and Dysynni, meet.

At the top of a slight incline, follow the track as it opens up onto a bracken-rich hillside. Pass a wooden stile and gate and continue downstream.

Take care along this stretch of the walk as there are steep drops down into the ravine with a fast-flowing river below you.

All along the river bank you'll pass ancient oak trees.

The track now becomes a mixture of stone, grass and mud and as you round the corner you'll be greeted by a wonderful view of the steep-sided valley ahead. To your right is an old white farmhouse, complete with a swing over the river below.

4. Cow rings and trough: SH 671071

A little further on, you'll come to a rocky outcrop, where small iron rings have been embedded into the rock.

These were once used by local farm women to tether their cows, whilst milking and feeding them.

One of the rocks has even been chiselled out to make a feeding trough for the cattle.

Follow the track down along the valley and through a wooden gate. The steep hillsides were covered in rusty-coloured bracken in October, and it gets noticeably cooler as the sun dips down behind the hills.

Keep an eye out for odd-shaped white rocks on the opposite side of the river bank, probably deposited there during the last Ice Age. One in particular resembles a standing stone and is easily spotted.

After a few minutes walking you'll arrive at a metal gate and stile. Head through this and continue down the valley.

Near the river, the track turns muddier as streams run off the hillsides down into the valley below, but you'll quickly return to steadier footing.

As the path straightens out, you'll find yourself walking through a marshy area, over a small stream and up past some rusting farm machinery in amongst the reeds.

5. Valley views: SH 662075

The river begins to widen at this point and there are some lovely

wooded areas before the walk opens up into the neighbouring valley, with some spectacular views towards Foel Caerberllan and Castell y Bere.

6. Stone wall: SH 660078

Walk towards a nearby house with an ornate stone wall and cross Pont Ystumanner, an old stone bridge. Take care as you're now walking on a well-used but narrow road.

Turn right after the bridge **(SH 660079)** and walk up to the crossroads. Turn right again and follow the signs for Abergynolwyn and Tal-y-llyn. From here head towards the impressive Caerberllan farmhouse.

7. Caerberllan farmhouse: SH 663078

This amazing building, built in 1590, has an infamous history of murder and family feuds, and has been owned by the same family for generations.

There are some lovely views from

here and the local farmer is a champion shire horse breeder, so you might see some of his show horses in the surrounding fields.

You might encounter the odd farm dog along this stretch, but their bark is worse than their bite. Wander down past the farmhouse and outbuildings and follow a rough vehicle track that skirts the foot of Foel Caerberllan.

There are some lovely old trees along this section of the walk including a magnificent holly tree covered in red berries in the autumn. After 10 minutes or so, the stony base of the nearby castle will appear ahead **(SH 668083)**.

There are a couple of tracks veering off left towards the main road, but keep straight on until you come to a kissing gate beneath a large, well-established tree.

Once through the gate, veer right and walk diagonally across the field until you reach a stile and signpost opposite the castle.

8. Castell y Bere: SH 668086

This impressive fortress, perched high on a rocky spur, has commanding views over the valley below and typifies the style of castle built by the Welsh princes.

It was begun by Llywelyn the Great in 1221 but captured by Edward I and his English army in 1283.

The gravel track up to the castle soon turns to tarmac and is fairly steep, so take your time.

The path spirals up and around into the castle entrance in the form of some steep wooden steps. The ruins are impressive and well worth a look. The views from the top are also spectacular at sunset.

9. Mary Jones's Chapel (St Michael's Church): SH 671089

Walk back down from the castle and veer left along the road down towards St Michael's Church at Llanfihangel-y-Pennant.

In 1800, a young girl by the name of Mary Jones walked 26 miles (barefoot!) from the village to Bala to buy a copy of the Bible in Welsh. This remarkable feat led to the formation of the British and Foreign Bible Society.

As you leave the church, head up the track opposite passing well-maintained public toilets (with disabled access).

The tarmac road soon gives way to a narrow and overgrown grassy track, which passes an old stone cottage on your right.

Castell y Bere

10. Oak forest: SH 675088

At the end of the track is a stile, adjacent to a derelict building with the river directly in front of you. Turn left and head towards a lovely oak tree, complete with yellow waymarker.

Keeping the river on your right, head up a winding, grassy track beneath the oak trees, listening out for sounds of a nearby waterfall.

The track here is a little confusing to follow as it branches off in a couple of directions, so just keep right and you should be fine.

After a few minutes you'll pass a rocky escarpment opposite a magnificent waterfall.

The path can be slippery, so watch your step along here and avoid any moss-covered rocks. Go over the stile and follow the track up into the field.

The route now follows a flat track with bracken and woodland on your left and hills to your right. There's an alternative path to your right but continue straight on.

The track can be fairly muddy here, especially after heavy rain, as you pass through low-lying marshland, so tread carefully.

The marshland ends at a field where there's a large stone that has been split in two.

11. Split rock: SH 678087

Take a look and see if you can spot the local farmers' graffiti, where they've carved their names into the rock.

You'll now follow an impressive valley all the way down to Abergynolwyn, with Foel Caerberllan on your right and Mynydd Tyn-y-fach to your left.

Nant-yr-Eira is the small stream which runs the entire length of this valley.

Old stone walls

12. Old stone boundary walls: SH 685086

Wander down through luscious green fields and across a small mountain stream. Just around the corner lies a derelict house.

All around you are beautifully crafted stone walls which mark field boundaries that climb up and over the mountain tops. Cross over the stile in the wall and continue up into the heart of the valley.

Towards the top you'll be rewarded with breathtaking views of the nearby mountains – Mynydd Cedris and Mynydd Rugog that keep watch over Tal-y-llyn below.

As you reach the top of the valley, you'll encounter more stone walls and a working sheep-pen **(SH 688083)**.

This is a great spot to take a breather and to look back down the valley at the track you've just followed. In the corner of the main boundary wall to your right is a stile.

13. Views over the Bala Fault: SH 688082

Climb over the stile and admire the views across the valley, which follows the Bala Fault. Waterfalls are to be seen in the distance. From here, the path turns into a rough vehicle track and heads downhill **(SH 689083)**.

The track is well marked and a yellow waymarker guides you to the right through an oak woodland, Coed Cedris. Take your time through this section as the path is steep and winding, and there are plenty of tree roots and tussocks to trip you up.

After a short walk you'll arrive at some fields. Be a little cautious here, especially if you have a dog, as there could be cattle in the field.

Walk across the field towards a stone boundary wall and gate on the left hand side of the field **(SH 693082)**.

Climb over the gate and turn right, following a country lane and the River Dysynni, back to the village.

15. The river path: SH 677074

After approximately half a mile, you'll notice a signpost near a house, directing you off the road, to the left.

Follow a steep and narrow track down to the river, taking in various steps and stiles as you go. The path gradually takes you down to the river, where you'll arrive at a muddy track which levels out and becomes marshy underfoot.

16. Pont y Cwrt: SH 675071

It's now a short walk along the river to a pretty stone bridge known as Pont y Cwrt.

Head through a gate up onto the main road and turn left, crossing over the bridge as you make your way back down Llanegryn Street, with the chapel and quarrymen's cottages now on your right.

At the end of the road, cross over near the Railway Arms and head up the hill past the Post Office and back through the woods to Nant Gwernol railway station to complete this circular walk.

Pont y Cwrt

Derek says. . .

THIS REALLY IS a cracking walk, and I'm not just saying that because I'm from Barry. It's packed with great views, wonderful beaches, lots of history and a lovely country park as well.

At the end of the walk, you can even give your feet a rest and catch a train back to the start. What more could you want? Well, dry weather would be nice, but this walk can be done come rain or shine.

For me, it was a trip down memory lane which brought back fond childhood memories of days spent on the beach or swimming in the pool at Cold Knap, now sadly filled in and grassed over.

It's amazing how much Barry has changed over the years. The Romans and Vikings were here. Much later, David Davies put Barry on the map by building his docks. By 1913 Barry was the largest coal-exporting port in the world!

The steam trains and Butlin's holiday camp may have long gone, but the TV show *Gavin and Stacey* has helped put the town back on the map. I can't guarantee that you'll bump into Nessa or Uncle Bryn on this walk but I hope you enjoy it as much as I do.

2. Barry Docks to Rhoose Point

Jackson's Bay

Approximate distance: 8 miles

Barry Docks to Rhoose Point

Start

served. Ordnance Survey Licence number 100019855

Distance: *8 miles*
Map: *OS Explorer Map 151*
Introduction: *This 8 mile linear walk along the coast to Porthkerry Country Park and Rhoose Point, takes you to the southernmost point on the mainland of Wales. It's a long but relatively easy walk with only a few hilly sections and plenty of places to rest. The cliffs along this part of Wales are spectacular and there is a wealth of maritime and natural history all along the coast – not to mention a couple of great sandy beaches at Barry Island.*

1. Start of the walk – Barry Docks railway station: ST 123678

The walk begins at Barry Docks railway station, near the Docks Offices where you'll find an impressive statue of David Davies **(ST 122676)**.

Davies, who hailed from Llandinam, was a Welsh industrialist and Liberal politician who sat in the House of Commons between 1874 and 1886 and was responsible for the construction of the docks at Barry.

He subsequently became very rich and his granddaughters, who inherited much of his wealth, collected many valuable French Impressionist paintings which can now be seen in the National Museum of Wales in Cardiff.

2. Waterfront walk: ST 120675

Cross the busy road of Ffordd y Mileniwm and turn left onto the new waterfront development with its modern wooden-clad housing and flats overlooking the water.

Follow the road up to the roundabout and turn left, passing through a tall yellow/black-striped security gate along Powell Duffryn Way and up the steep steps leading to Clive Road.

Turn left onto Clive Road in an easterly direction, turning right at the end into Clive Place. Head along Plymouth Road and take a left turn at Friar's Road.

3. St Baruc's Chapel: ST 119667

The nearby St Baruc's Chapel, tucked away in a fenced-off wooded area, has an interesting tale associated with it.

Saint Baruc apparently drowned when his boat overturned on a trip back from Flat Holm Island.

His body was washed ashore here and was buried up on the headland, a site subsequently visited by many pilgrims in medieval times.

Entrance to Barry Docks

It's been suggested that Barry takes its name from Baruc, who was actually an Irishman and patron saint of Cork. The jury is still out on that one.

4. Jackson's Bay: ST 121667

Veer left and follow the trail down past Barry Yacht Club and along the pristine sands of Jackson's Bay (where you'll find public toilets) towards a concrete walkway at the far end.

This secluded beach must be one of Barry's best-kept secrets, with its golden sands, sheltered location and pleasant views.

There's some interesting geology along this stretch of the walk and as you reach the path, you'll notice round freshwater pools on the ground to your right.

These have been formed by water washing down from natural springs above the cliffs and eroding holes in the softer rocks below.

Follow the path and you'll be rewarded with blustery sea views across to north Devon and the islands of Flat Holm and Steep Holm in the Bristol Channel.

5. Coastguard station: ST 120662

Continue along the footpath above the rocks on the far side of Jackson's Bay, past the Coastguard look-out station at Nell's Point and along to Barry Island's promenade.

The Butlin's holiday camp, built on Nell's Point and opened in 1966, was the last one ever to be built. The camp had more than 800 chalets and could accommodate nearly 5,000 visitors.

It closed in 1996 and the site was eventually demolished to make way for new housing and a recreational area.

6. Barry Island Beach: ST 114665

As the town of Barry expanded in the 1880s, Barry Island was joined to the mainland by a raised causeway. It was quickly developed as a resort and its funfair became renowned in Wales for its kiss-me-quick atmosphere, fairground rides, cafés and arcades.

Keep an eye out for Marco's Café which featured regularly in the BBC comedy series, *Gavin and Stacey*. Here you will find life-size

Whitmore Bay at Barry Island

cardboard cut-outs of the stars and you can even get a guided tour of the locations featured in the series.

At the western end of the beach follow a path leading to the old harbour. If you fancy a stroll to the headland, follow the path to the left.

7. Friar's Point: ST 111660

The headland here is a Site of Special Scientific Interest (SSSI) and is one of the best examples of a calcareous, cowslip-dominated hay meadow in south-east Wales.

The site is also a habitat for a variety of invertebrates, including bees, hoverflies, butterflies, grasshoppers and other insects.

The uneven ground here is all that remains of a medieval pillow mound, where rabbits were kept and bred as an important source of food.

Walk back to the path and continue towards the old harbour. Behind the ship's mast (an art installation) is an impressive old house, which was Barry's first hotel – the Marine Hotel – used as an army HQ during the Second World War.

Walk to the end of the track and turn right following the path to the harbour **(ST 108664)**, which flourished during the 16th and 17th centuries.

The next stop on the walk is Watch-tower Bay, but to get there you need to walk right around the old harbour and across the causeway.

8. Crossing the causeway: ST 113667

Walk along the side of the old harbour, through the car parking area, up the steps beside the Harbour Road Bridge and cross the causeway.

Turn left at The Parade, then turn left again into Cold Knap Way and walk down the footpath past an old thatched farmhouse.

9. Watch-tower Bay: ST 104663

Here you'll find the watch-tower which once marked the entrance to

this busy port. It was also used to store signal rockets.

10. Barry Lido: ST 102662

Walk across the former site of Barry Lido, where Derek once swam as a boy but which was later demolished and landscaped. All that remains are the shapes of the old changing rooms in the grass.

Turn left up the steps and walk along the promenade. The ornamental lake here is built in the shape of a harp, which you can see when flying into Cardiff Airport.

11. Cold Knap: ST 101663

This pebble beach has always been popular with sun seekers in summer and fishermen during winter, and you can find remains of a large Roman building dating from 290 AD on the bank behind the Knap car park.

The pebble beach extends for some way below the cliff, but we are heading up above the shoreline. At the car-park entrance roundabout (**ST 099665**; Knap Car Terrace), bear right and follow a track for 200 yards leading up in front of the houses and flats on the hillside.

12. Head towards the Golden Steps: ST 096668

Continue up a steep track to a grassy area at the top and follow the clifftop path for around ½ mile, with Marine Drive on your right.

At the far end, you'll arrive at a small entranceway leading you into woodland and the Porthkerry Country Park.

13. The Golden Steps: ST 091668

The woodland walk eventually brings you to the Golden Steps, which are not golden at all but were placed here by Lord Romilly. Local stories suggest that he laid a gold sovereign under the foundations during their construction.

In the woods here you'll find the rare purple gromwell, white wood anemone and a wealth of wildlife, including adders, woodpeckers, bats and the odd peregrine falcon.

14. Porthkerry Country Park: ST 087667

Porthkerry Country Park is a picturesque park overlooked by an impressive railway viaduct, built in the 1890s to carry coal to Barry Docks.

The Romilly family owned this country estate and sold it to the local council in 1929 and it's been a public park ever since.

At the bottom of the Golden Steps, turn right and continue along the pebble beach for around 200 yards until you come to a waymarker for the coastal path.

Bear right and head up a winding track leading you through a pretty deciduous woodland until you arrive at the bottom of a field, near the airport.

15. Bulwarks Camp: ST 081664

This field is actually the site of a fairly substantial Iron Age settlement known as the Bulwarks Camp but, other than a slight rise

Porthkerry Country Park

in the field, there's not much left of it to see.

The defended camp was probably occupied between 2000 BC and 75 AD, before the Romans arrived in south Wales.

Don't be surprised if planes pass low overhead at this point as the walking route passes directly underneath the flight path for Cardiff International Airport.

16. Porthkerry Caravan Park: ST 080663

Follow a grassy track, which cuts across the field diagonally in a northwesterly direction, towards the caravan park. As you enter the caravan park, keep left and follow the road running parallel with the sea.

Fans of the BBC comedy *Gavin and Stacey* may recognise some of the static caravans here which were used during the series for filming Nessa's home.

After approximately 400 yards, turn right towards Lower Quarry on the road skirting the caravan park and follow it around until, facing the sea, it drops down to Lower Quarry.

At the end of the road there are some good views looking back over the Knap at Barry and the Bristol Channel.

17. Heading towards Rhoose Point: ST 075660

Turn right onto a small footpath running parallel to the road you've just walked down, then turn left into a field leading towards the coastal path.

Stay on the path along this stretch as the cliffs, although beautiful to look at, are very dangerous and prone to rock slides.

After ⅓ mile or so you'll arrive at some steep steps. At the bottom, there's a nice little cove to the left – a slight detour that takes you closer to the water's edge.

Back on the main trail, climb up the steps and onto a long and narrow pathway, sheltered by hedgerows and with wild flowers on either side.

Follow this path for a further ⅓ mile towards Rhoose Point. On your right you'll see some man-made pools, a relic of the old stone quarry **(ST 075660)**.

These days the pools are a sanctuary for wildlife and support a whole range of birds, mammals, plants and insects. It's incredible to see what has developed here since the quarry closed in 2000.

Sea cliffs at Roose Point

Approaching Rhoose Point, you might spot what appear to be strange stone circles in the ground **(ST 066656)**. Rest assured, no alien activity has taken place: the artwork was placed here when the site was landscaped.

There are plenty more shapes too, including a compass and various snail-shaped squiggles, which can only be properly appreciated from the air, so take a look at the area on online aerial maps.

18. Rhoose Point: ST 065656

Rhoose Point (Trwyn y Rhŵs) is the most southerly point of mainland Wales.

As you approach the impressive stone circle and four-metre obelisk, you'll spot equally impressive natural cliffs to your left, which look as if they're guarding an ancient portal into the underworld.

The layered limestone cliffs here are spectacular and incredibly photogenic in the late afternoon sun. The area is also littered with fossils and huge, round stones.

Rhoose Point

Take care if you venture onto the beach as the ground is uneven. It's best also to avoid standing too near to the bottom of the cliffs as they can be prone to rockfalls.

If you walk up past the stone circle onto the clifftop, you'll get nice views along the coast to Aberthaw. It's also well worth taking time to explore the lagoon area, which is full of wild orchids and other rare plants.

19. End of the walk – Rhoose railway station: ST 062662

Follow a winding track northwards towards the houses and turn left onto a narrow tarmac path. Follow this to the top of the hill and turn left into Heol y Pentir, the road which leads to Rhoose railway station.

Here you can catch regular trains back to Barry and Cardiff or – if you're feeling really fit – you can walk back!

Derek says. . .

THIS BEAUTIFUL WALK in the Rhondda valley is within easy reach of Cardiff and Swansea, and close to the Brecon Beacons.

This hike through history takes you on an Indiana Jones style adventure to the summit of Pen Pych, past cascading waterfalls, former industrial landscapes, and shady pine forests to the source of the River Rhondda.

The impressive 'table mountain' of Pen Pych is more than 1,400 feet high. It's a great place to come and watch the world go by, and the views of Treherbert and the valley below are amazing.

When the industry was at its peak, there were about 66 coalmines in the Rhondda, the most intensely mined area in Britain, if not the world. You can still see signs of the former coal industry but much of the land has since been reclaimed and is now green again.

This is a varied walk through a fascinating landscape shaped by glaciers during the last Ice Age. After a day of heavy rain, the waterfalls are always impressive. And don't forget the annual Valleys Walking Festival in September, which organises walks to suit everyone.

3. Blaencwm

Viewpoint over Treherbert

Approximate distance: 6 miles

Distance: 6 miles

Map: *OS Explorer 166 – Rhondda & Merthyr Tydfil.*

Introduction: *This moderate 6 mile circular walk takes you up into the heart of the Rhondda valley, from Blaencwm to the impressive table-top mountain of Pen Pych. Following the course of the River Rhondda and its gushing waterfalls, you'll pass into deep pine forests, across moorland and through an Iron Age settlement before dropping back into Blaencwm. As you enjoy those panoramic green views it may be difficult to imagine that this was once one of the most heavily industrialised areas in Britain, if not the world.*

Trail towards the pine forests

1. Start of the walk – Pen Pych woodland car park: SS 924991

This walk begins in the car park – check car park opening and closing times before setting off, just in case the site is locked when you return.

At the far end of the car park you'll find a zigzagging trail leading up into the pine forests **(SS 925992)**.

All around you are vast conifer forests blanketing the pockmarked hillsides and valleys where the coalmining industry once thrived.

Make your way up a stone track, laced with bracken on either side, meandering in and out of forest clearings. You will cross several small mountain streams as you go.

Approximately ½ mile along the track you'll pass a pleasant picnic area with lovely views.

A little further on you'll encounter your first waterfall, next to a viewing area.

2. Waterfalls: SS 918994

The path is considerably steeper from this point on and a muddy trail is replaced by a stone track leading up to an impressive waterfall cascading over a high cliff.

The area directly in front of the waterfall is strewn with large boulders, so take care if you wish to gain a closer look. Next bear right and continue up a stone track hugging the hillside, all the way to the top of Pen Pych **(SS 922994)**.

At the top, you'll have a bird's eye view of the surrounding valleys and might even be able to spot where an old railway tunnel used to run into the side of the mountain, before emerging in the Afan valley.

Because the grass hereabouts is tussocky, it's easy to fall over, so watch your step. There's not a lot in the way of wildlife up here but ravens and buzzards can be seen soaring high with the aid of thermals.

Continue along a marked walking trail, passing more conifer plantations on your left hand side and head towards a fence and area of rough grassland.

3. Views over Treherbert: SS 923996

The track veers left but if you turn right and follow the fence-line down, you'll be rewarded with

another viewpoint on the tip of Pen Pych, overlooking Treherbert and the valley below.

4. The route from Pen Pych: SS 921997

Retrace your steps back to the track and walk in a northwesterly direction, keeping the valley to your right and the conifer trees on your left.

Depending on the weather, it can be pretty bleak up here with only the occasional 'croak' from a raven for company, but it does have a certain rugged charm all of its own. The grasses either side of the track are long and knee-deep in places but the track itself is well maintained and cut to a good length for walking.

5. Old stone wall: SS 920999

Within about ⅓ mile you'll come to an old stone boundary wall. Turn right and follow a rough track, flanked by heather, down into a deep conifer-clad valley.

The route here is more sheltered beneath the steep cliffs and scars of Craig Blaenrhondda. Enter the dark and dense conifer forests to your right.

6. Enter the pine forests: SS 920004

It's eerily quiet along this section. The ground is carpeted with vibrant green mosses, whilst lichen smothers the lower hanging tree branches, giving the landscape an almost Nordic feel.

Keep an eye out for some unusual rock strata and wonderfully crafted ancient stone walls here, where the lines between man-made and natural features have become blurred over time.

The next section of the track can be incredibly boggy, especially after rainfall, so if you're planning on doing this walk in autumn or winter, a pair of decent waterproof walking boots are essential.

Make your way along the track, towards a wider, fairy-tale forest path. Pay attention as you exit the forest, as the track forks in two different directions.

There is a small, standing stone (route marker) here, which can be hard to spot. Turn left and follow a muddy track up the hill where two mountain streams flow down either side of the trail **(SN 920007)**.

The ground here can be wet and slippery as streams flow down from the hillsides above. Follow the track up to the next forested area, again carpeted with mosses and lichens and the odd boundary wall dating back to the 18th century.

Leaving the woods, you'll arrive at a rocky clearing with views over the A4061 Rhigos Road running down through the valley.

As you walk down the hill, you might be able to pick out an Iron Age settlement in the distance, which you'll get a better view of later.

The track down can be wet and boggy as the path follows a stream bed through a small, marshy area, so tread carefully if you want to keep your socks dry.

A little further on, you'll get your first glimpse of the River Rhondda, complete with waterfall and a metal footbridge **(SN 922015)**.

Apparently there's an old steam engine boiler at the bottom of the falls, which was left behind after the mines closed.

7. Crossing the River Rhondda: SN 922015

Cross the metal footbridge, which can be slippery in the rain, and turn left following a waymarker.

Head up the valley along a narrow, grassy track, clambering over rocks and heather. Keep the river on your left and pass a large boulder field on your right.

This section of the walk is incredibly scenic and makes a nice change from all the conifer forests. Old stone walls, overhanging trees and a fast-flowing river are a visual treat but what lies ahead is even more spectacular.

Pass through the old iron gateway **(SN 919017)**. A little further on you'll come to a narrow concrete walkway crossing the river. Take the crossing and follow the track down through an ornate, rusting iron fence and gate towards a footbridge spanning the river, and cross back over the river.

8. Nant Melyn waterfall: SN 918017

A little further on you'll arrive at a pristine pond. The stunning Nant Melyn waterfall cascades into it at the far end.

If you're feeling daring, you can cross the weir here via a concrete walkway.

Nant Melyn

Once across, you can get a closer look at the pond and waterfall. It's also a nice spot to eat lunch.

Retrace your footsteps to the iron gate and pass through a gap in the fence. Walk up the valley following the Nant Garreg Lwyd river.

The terrain can be a bit tricky with long grasses, soft ground, odd-shaped boulders and damp ground underfoot. There are no obvious waymarkers but you can clearly see where other walkers have been before you.

9. Rocky steps: SN 919019

A little further on at the end of the track, you'll arrive at a waymarker near a rocky hillside. Head up the stone steps. Turn right and make your way up a steep, winding track through the heather. About halfway up, besides another waymarker, there are good views back down the valley.

Hendre'r Mynydd settlement

Continue up through the grassland towards the A4061, Rhigos Road. You could end your walk here at the kissing gate **(SN 922020)**. There's a car park opposite, where you could leave a car or arrange to be picked up. Take care crossing the road, as there's a nasty bend at this point.

To continue, bear right and follow a trail downhill towards the Iron Age settlement of Hendre'r Mynydd.

10. Hendre'r Mynydd Iron Age settlement: SN 923019

The remains are extensive and although the walls are low, you can clearly see where the circular stone buildings once stood. Quite why anyone would want to farm up here is anyone's guess, as the ground is sloping, barren and rocky!

The valley widens here, offering stunning views over the sites of the former Blaenrhondda Colliery (North Dunraven Pit) and Fernhill Colliery **(SN 925010)**.

The flatter, greener area in the middle ground was home to a Wild West theme park in the 1980s – hard to imagine now.

Follow a gently sloping, stony track

down below the road, stepping over occasional mountain streams. You'll also find the odd car wreck here – insurance scams apparently. The more inaccessible ones have been left and now provide shelter for the local wildlife.

All along here you'll find signs of the former coal industry, such as slag heaps and the odd lump of Rhondda coal.

From up here you can see much of the route you've already walked, as well the River Rhondda and waterfall below that was previously hidden from view **(SN 926016)**.

The track now heads up a slight incline where you'll find yourself walking through what resembles a quarry with rocks strewn on either side of the track.

Despite the area's scarred terrain, nature does flourish here. Kestrels, buzzards and the occasional feral goat can all be seen, as well as wild flowers and butterflies in summer.

11. Rhigos Road watchman's hut: SN 928013

If you veer left and cross the main road, you'll notice an old brick hut on the side of the road. A watchman was once employed to clear rocks from the road here following landslides.

Nowadays the cliffs are lined with metal gauze to prevent rocks from falling onto the road, but the old hut remains.

The watchman also collected rubbish and created a garden of colourful trees and flowers made from discarded plastic, behind his hut. Local school children have continued his work, adding to the unusual display.

Return to the trail and you'll find the track splits in two **(SN 929007)**.

Follow the track that hugs the road and head down the hill crossing over a stream as you go.

12. Coldra Road: SN 929003

The trail leads down onto a dirt road (marked as Coldra Road on OS maps) that snakes its way down to the nearby town of Treherbert, lying in the shadow of Pen Pych.

Along the road, another track appears ahead of you. Ignore this and keep left, following the bend around and down towards houses.

Watchman's hut

Turn left and descend the concrete steps that are marked with waymarker points **(SN 928002)**. At the bottom of the steps follow a grassy trail that leads to Cross Brook Street and a return to civilisation.

Turn left into Brook Street and continue for approximately ½ mile **(SN 927001)**.

13. End of the walk – Graig y Ddelw: SS 928992

Turn right and walk behind the nearby houses of Graig y Ddelw. Follow a grassy track back **(SS 924991)**, turning right into the car park where the walk began.

The Coldra Road track winds through the former industrial ladscape

Derek says. . .

I REALLY ENJOYED this walk which starts in sunny Penarth at the entrance to Cardiff Bay. It can be blustery on the barrage but the views across the city and the Bristol Channel are wonderful.

There are lots of things to do and see along the way, including historic landmarks, such as the Norwegian Church, and iconic buildings like the Wales Millennium Centre and the Senedd. And the Doctor Who Experience is a must if you're a fan!

On the barrage, stop and have a look at the fish pass. Salmon from the River Taff have been known to travel as far as Greenland before returning to Cardiff Bay.

This circular route is now possible since the opening of the Pont y Werin footbridge. The Cardiff Bay Wetlands Reserve is great for bird-spotting, and provides an escape from the crowds in Mermaid Quay.

When I filmed this walk for television, I did it using walking poles. They took some getting used to, but Nordic walking is a great way of keeping fit, giving your legs and upper body a good workout.

So, if you fancy doing this walk, why not do it the Nordic way and discover the delights of the Bay.

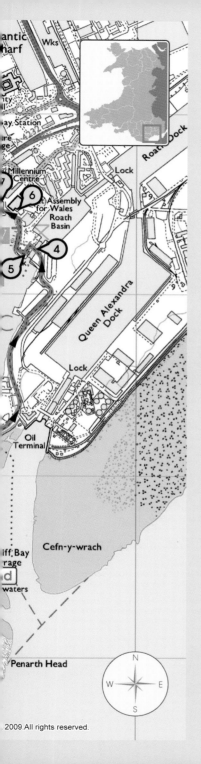

Cardiff Bay

Approximate distance: 5 miles

Great Welsh Walks

Distance: 5 miles
Map: *OS Explorer Map 151*
Introduction: *This easy 5 mile circular walk around Cardiff Bay takes in the area's iconic landmarks as well as some you may not be so familiar with. The walk begins at the Custom House in Penarth and crosses the barrage. It then loops around Mermaid Quay before heading through a nature reserve and across the River Ely to Cardiff Bay Yacht Club. From there it's a short walk over the footbridge to Penarth, through the marina to the finish. As it's a circular walk you can really start wherever you want along the route, or do half and catch a water taxi back to your starting point.*

1. Start of the walk – Custom House: ST 123678

The walk begins at the Custom House situated beneath Penarth Head at the bottom of Paget Road. If you're arriving by car, there is a pay and display car park opposite.

Head onto the barrage locks and you'll notice huge yellow paint markings. At this stage all you'll see is yellow paint daubed over various parts of the lock but a little further on, all is revealed.

2. Optical art: ST 190726

Walk along the pavement to the third lock and you'll notice a yellow X painted on the ground.

Standing on the mark, look towards

Optical art

the lock and, if in the right position, you'll find that the yellow paint joins up to reveal a series of perfect concentric circles. This optical-effect art installation is called *3 Ellipses for 3 Locks* and is by the Swiss artist, Felice Varini.

After the last lock, turn left towards the fish pass. There are toilets located here.

3. Fish pass: ST 191727

The fish pass here is used by Atlantic salmon and sea trout (sewin). Freshwater flows down from the bay into the pass and out to sea. The fish

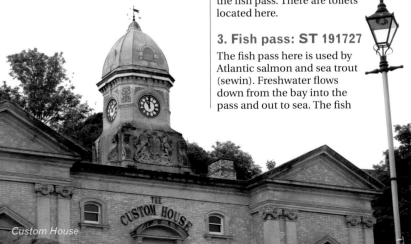

Custom House

recognise the water of their home rivers and follow it up through the pass to spawn.

Continue along an exposed section of the barrage, open to the full force of the wind from the Bristol Channel. Follow the path through a coastal landscaped area, past two white sails **(ST 191732)** that stand in the middle of the barrage and which add a nice nautical feel to the area.

Continue on to a children's playground and skatepark next to the Watersports Activity Centre. The path then skirts through the old docks area.

Up ahead, you'll see a large blue, futuristic looking building which is the home of the 'Doctor Who Experience'. Here you can help the Doctor escape from his foes, fly the Tardis and come face-to-face with some of the scariest monsters seen on screen.

Doctor Who is actually made in the BBC drama village, at Roath Lock Studios nearby **(ST 195741)**.

The studios now provide a perm-anent, purpose-built home for dramas including *Casualty*, *Pobol y Cwm*, *Doctor Who* and *Wizards versus Aliens*.

4. Porth Teigr Outer Lock Crossing: ST 194742

Keep left and cross over the red metal bridge) – known locally as the 'Origami Bridge' – and walk towards the Norwegian Church.

5. Scott Antarctic Memorial and Norwegian Church: ST 194742

Approaching the Norwegian Church, you'll see a rather striking white statue depicting Captain Scott and his team.

The statue by local sculptor Jonathan Williams features a white

and blue mosaic, suggesting the Antarctic ice, and depicts Scott and his men trapped in the snow as they head towards the South Pole.

The rear section of the statue reveals the foresails of the expedition's vessel, the *Terra Nova*, which sailed from here in June 1910. Scott was beaten to the South Pole by the Norwegian explorer, Roald Amundsen.

The church, established in 1868, was built to provide religious and social care for the thousands of Norwegian sailors employed by the Norwegian merchant fleet. Its original location was between the East and West Docks (near the present day Senedd building).

Having fallen into disrepair, the church was rescued by the Norwegian Church Preservation Trust in 1987 and carefully dismantled, moved and re-erected on its new site.

Today, there's a thriving café inside, perfect for when the weather turns sour.

One of the aims of Cardiff Bay's development was to create a vast open-air art gallery with public sculptures. Keep an eye out for some of the artworks for which the Bay is now famous.

Continue past a walled area with sea creatures carved into it **(ST 194744)**.

The praying figure at the end is the the World Harmony Peace Statue.

Ahead of you, outside the Senedd, is a remarkable sculpture, which is actually a face in the shape of a boat's hull – the Merchant Seafarers' War Memorial.

6. The Senedd: ST 193745

The Senedd building opened in 2006 and houses the Welsh Assembly debating chamber and committee rooms. It is also a public building, so feel free to use the toilets and café located inside.

Designed by Richard Rogers, it's said to be one of the most environmentally-friendly parliament buildings in the world. It is built from mainly Welsh materials – including 1,000 tonnes of Welsh slate. The curving red-cedar roof is meant to represent the waves in the bay.

The wind cowl on the top of the roof rotates, drawing warm air up and out of the debating chamber below.

7. Pierhead Building: ST 193745

This Grade One listed terracotta building next door to the Senedd is

part of the National Assembly and houses a visitor centre.

Originally the headquarters of the Bute Dock Company, it was taken over by the Port of Cardiff in the 1940s. It's now a free museum and visitor centre, displaying the history of the docks and Welsh devolution.

The building incorporates a Gothic design, complete with hexagonal chimneys, carved friezes, gargoyles, and an ornamental clock tower, known as 'Baby Big Ben'.

From here, walk around the back of the building and turn left down some steps that lead into Roald Dahl Plass.

8. Roald Dahl Plass: ST 192745

Named after Cardiff-born writer, Roald Dahl, this bowl-shaped plaza is a popular amphitheatre for events throughout the year, including open-air concerts and cultural activities.

The basin was formerly West Bute Dock when the bay was a thriving coal port. 'Plass' means 'plaza' in Norwegian, acknowledging the writer's roots and his Norwegian ancestry.

Pierhead Building

Wales Millennium Centre

At the end of the plaza is a 70ft high metallic sculpture, with a constant stream of water running down the side.

Sci-fi fans will recognise it here from the BBC *Doctor Who* spin-off series, *Torchwood*, which had its fictional base located beneath.

Behind the fountain is the striking Wales Millennium Centre, with its distinctive copper roof. The arts centre is dedicated to musical theatre, opera, ballet and dance, with the largest stage in Wales.

Head down to the waterfront, passing underneath a footbridge at the end of the pass.

On your right hand side are some Roman numerals carved into the side of the wall, which once marked the water-levels when this was a working dock. On the opposite side, you'll find a slate plaque commemorating Roald Dahl.

Turn right and continue along the boardwalk. When we were here we encountered a bizarre shrine dedicated to the dead fictional character, Ianto Jones, from *Torchwood*. Fans from around the world visit here and pin their messages of condolence to the wall **(ST 191744)**.

Continue up the ramp to Mermaid Quay with its bars and restaurants. Follow the waterfront around to its end and continue down past the former docks towards the Techniquest building.

Pass Techniquest and turn left near an old blue crane and walk along the edge of the far dock towards a red-brick building.

Walk up the steps and around the corner to the St Davids Hotel. Just before the hotel, turn left and head down some steps to a wooden boardwalk skirting the base of the hotel **(ST 190742)**.

Follow the boardwalk around to the other side and walk up the steps to a circular, stone sculpture featuring nesting birds **(ST 190741)**. Continue along the path and turn left down into the wetlands reserve.

9. Cardiff Bay Wetlands Reserve: ST 188741

This unlikely reserve was created in 2002 when the barrage was completed and the previous saline mudflats were transformed into a freshwater lake.

The reserve is now an important site for over-wintering and breeding birds and is popular with birdwatchers.

In summer, you are likely to spot familiar birds such as swans, grebes and warblers – but surprisingly there are also otters and water voles

This is the temporary home of the Cardiff Devils ice hockey team. There are plans for an exciting new ice arena to be built in the bay in the near future.

Beyond this is the impressive, glass-fronted Cardiff International Pool, with a 50 metre Olympic pool, seating for 1,000 spectators and a leisure pool with flumes. Walk past the pool, following signs for Penarth, and Cardiff International White Water.

here, though you'll be lucky if you see them.

The reserve is free to enter and is a wild green oasis in this urban landscape. At the far end is a wooden pontoon (**ST 186739**) providing excellent views over the bay and the wildfowl that live amongst the reeds.

Stepping back off the pontoon, turn left at the Cader Idris sculpture and continue along the path towards a roundabout near Cardiff Bay Yacht Club (**ST 186741**).

Walk straight across the roundabout and up along a path towards the busy A4232 road-bridge towards Penarth (**ST 186742**).

Turn left and walk across the River Taff bridge via a pedestrian path passing the various luxury flats that have sprung up in recent years.

At the bottom of the footpath, turn left and follow the signs for the International Sports Village. A little further on, before you reach the roundabout, turn left and walk up onto a wooden boardwalk to your right (**ST 181733**).

Take care along the boardwalk, as it can become very slippery when wet. This is a quiet section of the walk, with sweeping views over the bay and plenty of ducks in the water below for company.

After a short stroll, you'll notice a large blue building on your right.

10. Cardiff International White Water: ST 179728

This Olympic-standard white-water rafting centre opened in 2010 and has proved popular.

Here you can you try your hand at kayaking, canoeing or white-water rafting, or simply sit back and watch other people getting wet. The café has a balcony overlooking the water.

Continue along Watkiss Way, past Cardiff Marina and turn left down a narrow track leading onto Pont y Werin, which spans Cardiff Bay's second river – the Ely.

11. Pont y Werin: ST 177728

The footbridge, which opened in July 2010, was the final link in the chain connecting the bay to Penarth by bicycle and foot.

Sculptures at Pont y Werin

Pont y Werin means 'the People's Bridge' in Welsh and is an example of a bascule bridge – a moveable bridge providing clearance for large boats.

The transport charity, Sustrans, provided sculptures at the bridge featuring laser-cut outlines of local heroes, celebrities and historic figures. Here you'll find sculptures of Sybil Williams, the founder member of Pedal Power, and Cardiff Devils ice-hockey player, Jason Stone.

On the Penarth side, you'll find outlines of Paralympic gold medallist, Tanni Grey-Thompson and Olympic gold medallist, Nicole Cooke.

Cross over the bridge **(ST 177726)** and turn left along Marconi Avenue, following the path for around 300 yards.

Pass by some flats at Chandler's Quay and turn left onto a red-brick path, which takes you along the waterfront past John Bachelor's Way, with the barrage in the distance.

At the far end is a housing development known as Plas Taliesin. Follow a path through the houses to Penarth marina where you'll catch a glimpse of the former Custom House in the background, signalling the end of the walk.

Turn right and cross over a footbridge spanning the lock-gate to the other side of the marina **(ST 188725)**.

End of the walk – return to the Custom House: ST 189725

Pass the Marina Office and follow a narrow path to the end. Around the corner you'll see Custom House, and the end of the walk.

Penarth Marina

Derek says. . .

THERE MAY BE a nuclear power station close by, but don't let that put you off this walk. Anglesey is steeped in history, myths and legends, in addition to coves and stunning coastal views.

Cemaes Bay, the most northerly village in Wales, was a simple fishing village before it became an industrial port. It's now tranquil again with a lovely sandy beach. In the harbour, look out for the fully-restored Charles Henry Ashley lifeboat which operated between 1872 and 1932.

The walk involves a few ups and downs, but the climb from Porth Llanlleiana is worth the effort. The Edwardian watch-tower is also a great place to watch ships pass by as they battle the fierce tides.

Look out for the old brickworks at Porth Wen, and there are loads of seabirds including choughs and peregrines nesting on the cliffs. If you're lucky, you may even see the odd porpoise.

Pop into Llanbadrig Church which the Dalai Lama described as the 'most peaceful place on earth'.

Anglesey has 125 miles of coastal path and every June a walking festival is held, giving everyone an opportunity to see and learn about the treasures that this beautiful island has to offer.

5. Cemaes

Approximate distance: 8½ miles

Cemaes

Middle Mouse /
Ynys Badrig
(LLANBADRIG C)

Llanlleiana
Head

Porth
Llanlleiana

Hell's Mouth or
Porth Cynfor

Torllwyn

Trwynbychan

95

Dinas Gynfor

Porth
Adda

Llanlleiana

Graig
Wen
91

Porth Wen

Isle of Angl
Llwybr Arf

Shaft
(dis)

Trwyn
Llech

Cae Owen

Isallt

Bryn Llewelyn

Castell

Yr E

Cae Adda

Ty-du
57

Porthwen

Tyddyn
Rhydderch

Rhyd-y-clafdy

Bodhunoe

badrig

Neuadd

Spr

47

Rhos-isaf

Betws

53

Peibron

Refail
Bach

59

Tregynrig
Bach

LLANBADRIG C

Tregynrig
Fawr

Fawr
m

Wind Generators

Buarth-
y-foel

39

W

62

W

Spr

Nant-y-frân

93

d Generators

PpHo

Tyn-y-Gors

Fferm Wynt
Rhyd-y-groes
(Wind Farm)

Earthwork

67

N

Rhyd-y-groes

W   E

Per

Shop-y-goeden

S

92

Criw

FB

Hafodlin

served: Ordnance Survey Licence number 100019855

Great Welsh Walks

Distance: 8½ miles
Map: *OS Explorer Map: 262*
Introduction: *An 8½ mile circular walk along the rugged north coast of Anglesey with great sea views and several features of geological and historical interest. Starting near Wylfa Power Station, you'll pick up the Anglesey Coast Path along to the idyllic setting of Cemaes Bay, before continuing through remnants of the area's industrial past as you head towards Llanbadrig Church, one of the earliest Christian sites in Wales. From here, you'll be dazzled by the spectacular sea views as you make your way towards the former brickworks at Porth Wen, before picking up a quiet road taking you back to Cemaes.*

Wylfa Power Station

1. Start of the walk – Trwyn Yr Wylfa: SH 356938

The walk begins at a local wildlife reserve in the grounds of an old manor house, a stone's throw away from the power station.

As you leave the car park, turn right past the ruins and walk through a metal gate between two brick pillars, following the Anglesey Coast Path.

Continue along a rough track over grassland and through woods for around 130m. Walk up a sloping track and veer left, passing through a ruined stone wall that leads into the field bordering the power station.

Wylfa Nuclear Power Station is now the only nuclear power station left in Wales and has been supplying electricity to the National Grid since 1971.

Walk diagonally across a long grassy meadow with woods to your left and head through a gap in the field boundary.

2. Old Lifeboat station: SH 356942

Turn right and walk through a gap in a drystone wall, following the path down towards the sea, before turning right.

In the cove below is the former lifeboat station at Porth yr Ogof, named after the cave ('ogof' is Welsh for a cave) which can be seen on the small island behind the slipway.

As you follow the coast path, there are views of the Skerries lighthouse

to the west, Middle Mouse island to the north east and White Lady's Rock, which you can just make out below the cliffs at Llanbadrig.

The grassy track hereabouts is well-worn but full of wild flowers, from spotted orchids to thrift and vetch. And in summer, it's alive with insects and butterflies.

3. Wylfa Bay: SH 361937

Walk towards Wylfa Bay, following the hedge line as far as a wooden gate on your left. Head through the gate and across the field, passing the beach below.

The sheltered bay is an excellent swimming spot at high tide and was home to local swimming galas between the 1930s and 1960s.

Head along a narrow overgrown path – full of foxgloves and other wild flowers in summer – ignoring the metal kissing gate on your right and into an overgrown field.

The grassy track eventually leads onto a rough gravel road. After a further 200m, pass through a wide stone gateway and turn left, walking behind houses bordering the beach road.

Pass through a wooden gate and

Porth yr Ogof and remains of the lifeboat slipway

follow the path onto a tarmac track as far as a large stone house at Penrhyn, overlooking the bay.

At the house, turn right **(SH 369938)** and follow a narrow walled lane down between the houses, passing a pretty whitewashed cottage known as Viking's Cottage.

Look out for the unusual metal gate, complete with Viking helmet and swords. Turn left and follow the path down to the scenic Cemaes Bay, best seen at high tide **(SH 370937)**.

Follow the beach road for 300m as far as the harbour, passing a parking area with pretty coastal gardens and an old green buoy that used to mark the notorious Harry Furlong rocks near the Skerries. Turn left and head down into the harbour.

Cemaes harbour

4. Cemaes Harbour: SH 372936

Cemaes was originally a fishing village but during the 18th and 19th centuries developed into a thriving port exporting local limestone, marble and bricks. Its pier was extended in the 1800s by Ishmael Jones, a local sea captain.

You can spot his additions by the different shades of stonework. The harbour was recently purchased from the local council and is now managed by the locals.

You'll find the Charles Henry Ashley lifeboat here, unless it's out on a trip. Restored to its former glory at a cost of £100,000, it's now available for public use.

Head out of the harbour, turn right and walk up the hill past pretty coastal cottages. Opposite the Stag Inn is a left turn up a narrow alley-way behind a large yellow house next to the river.

Walk up the alley and turn left onto a blue road bridge spanning the river. In bygone days this area was a hive of activity as bricks were transported down river to the harbour, from a brickworks upstream.

Cross the bridge, proceed along Bridge Street and turn left, back down to the other side of the harbour. Here you'll find a turntable once used to turn the carts around after they'd delivered the bricks to the port.

Walk along the sea front past a car park and walk up the road a short way. Turn left, following a National Trust sign for Llanbadrig **(SH 375938)** and head along a steep muddy track up to the headland overlooking Cemaes Bay, with some outstanding views over the village and harbour.

Continue along the coast path, passing through a wooden gate. Head down the dip and back up the other side, passing a limekiln and former quarrying sites as you head towards White Lady's Rock, a favourite haunt of geologists.

The whole of Anglesey is a designated European Geopark and near here is one of the best places to see the Gwna Mélange, a mixture of very ancient rocks created by an enormous underwater landslide.

View towards White Lady's Rock

5. White Lady's Rock: SH 376944

This triangular-shaped, light grey slab of rock once formed part of a sea-arch but was sadly quarried in Victorian times for its quartz, used as shingle for pathways in private gardens.

Follow a narrow muddy track and steps down to a pebbled bay but, before you reach White Lady's Rock, turn right towards a wooden gate that leads to a tarmac road. Turn left and walk up the hill through a car park to what is possibly Wales's oldest Christian site.

Llanbadrig Church

6. Llanbadrig Church: SH 376946

Legend has it that Bishop Patrick (later Saint Patrick) was shipwrecked on Middle Mouse, the island opposite. He swam ashore and lived in Ogof Badrig, a cave at the foot of the cliffs, before building the church here in thanks to God for saving his life.

Inside the present day church you'll find unusual and ornate blue Islamic tiling around the altar.

Restoration of the church in 1884 was funded by Lord Henry Stanley, who had converted to Islam. He requested that his faith be represented inside, hence the blue tiling and beautiful geometric patterned stained glass. He later became the first Muslim member of the House of Lords.

The church also houses the Icthus Stone, a prehistoric standing-stone later inscribed with the Christian symbol of a fish.

Leaving the church, turn right and walk through a wooden kissing gate, following the cemetery wall around the church.

To the left, up on the headland, is a wooden bench where the Dalai Lama is said to have sat, declaring it to be 'the most peaceful place on earth'.

Follow the path as far as a wooden fence – it is below here that St Patrick's cave is located **(SH 376947)** but the path is steep and hazardous so we advise against using it. Remain on the coast path, passing through a wooden gate and following the fence line to your right.

Bear right and descend some steep wooden steps, following the curve of a stone wall on your right. Along this stretch of coast during the summer months, you can hear the seabirds squawking loudly over on Middle Mouse.

Climb a steep hill and pass through two more kissing gates, before dropping down more steps on your way to Porth Llanlleiana.

From the top of this section, you'll have nice views down over the hills beyond. You may also be able to

Islamic tiling in Llanbadrig Church

make out the location of an Iron Age promontory fort behind the watch-tower on Llanlleiana Head.

Follow the steps down into Porth Llanlleiana, a pretty, sheltered bay made up of small boulders.

7. Porth Llanlleiana: SH 388950

At the bottom of the steps, you'll find a ruined building and chimney, once used in the production of china clay.

It later became a hotel but the building burned to the ground in 1920 and has been left as a ruin ever since.

Nearby there was once a 7th century nunnery where Llywelyn the Great allegedly sent his unfaithful wife, Joan, for a year.

There's a picnic table here and it's a scenic place to stop for a snack. Llanlleiana means 'church of the nuns'.

Continue straight past the ruins and up a steep, zigzagging path towards a watch-tower on top of the headland. Your legs will be burning a little by the time you reach the top but the views from Dinas Gynfor are worth it.

The hillfort covers an impressive 50 acres and was named after a British Prince who landed here long ago. You can still clearly see the ramparts on the inland side of the fort.

8. Watch-tower: SH 389952

The watch-tower or summerhouse was built by a local sea captain to commemorate the coronation of Edward VII in 1902. It is thought that the captain used the tower during his retirement to watch the ships go by.

From the top you have stunning views of the Skerries, Middle Mouse, East Mouse, Point Lynas and, on a clear day, across to the Isle of Man, 70km to the north.

Leave the watch-tower, turn left and follow the ridge of the headland down the hill, passing Porth Cynfor with its scenic cliffs as you go.

Porth Llanlleiana

Cross over a wooden stile before climbing up a winding track with steep steps leading to the top of the hill. From there, follow a wide grassy track towards Porth Wen.

Here you'll find more evidence of the area's industrial past in the form of heavy winding gear used to lower quartzite – used in the production of silica bricks – from the quarries down to the brickworks below.

9. Porth Wen brickworks: SH 402946

Head down a grassy slope, lined with foxgloves in summer, into Porth Wen. The cove is stunning, especially at high tide, and is a popular spot for people to moor up their boats.

To your left you'll get your first glimpse of the former brickworks with its towering chimney stacks and beehive-shaped kilns. The brickworks supplied silica bricks – heat-resistant bricks used to line furnaces in the steel industry – and also produced glazed tiles for use in Victorian houses. Production ceased at the beginning of the First World War. The site is now derelict but still impressive. The bricks were exported from a small harbour alongside the works but it was never easy for large boats to dock here. Next to the harbour is a spectacular sea-arch.

Follow a grassy track to a fork and take the right hand track towards a metal gate.

Head up a narrow, overgrown trail **(SH 340945)** leading up past a rocky escarpment with views over the windfarm above Nant-y-Frân.

10. End of the walk – road back to Cemaes: SH 398942

Walk down past a farm gate to a minor road (Tŷ Du farm on your left) and turn right.

Follow a quiet winding road back to Cemaes passing Llanbadrig. Rejoin the coastal path as you make your way back to Wylfa Bay.

Walk past the bay (on your right hand side) towards the hedge line. Pass through the wooden gate **(SH 360937)** and walk straight across the field to the woods opposite, in the direction of the power station.

Pick up a short trail in the woods **(SH 357938)** and veer left, following the track to the road. Turn left and head back to the car park where you started the walk.

Porth Wen brickworks

Derek says. . .

OFFA'S DYKE has been listed amongst the top 10 great wall walks in the world, and I'm not surprised. It passes through eight different counties and crosses the border more than 25 times, so it's possible to have one foot in Wales and the other in England!

If you fancy a challenge, the whole trail of 177 miles can be done in a couple of weeks. A lot of people do it in bite-size chunks, and this walk is a good taster which you can easily do in a day.

The dyke is an amazing earthwork with lots of ups and downs. It was built to protect Mercia against attacks from Powys and parts of it are still quite high, even after 1,200 years of wear and tear.

Offa's Dyke is brimming with wild flowers, birds, butterflies and mammals, including badgers, and you may even spot a red grouse hiding in the heather.

This particular walk follows the dyke from Churchtown to the historic market town of Montgomery with its wood-framed houses and cobbled streets. After a quick cappuccino, you're ready for the final hike up to Montgomery Castle, with magnificent views and a fitting spot to end a walk in the Marches.

6. Churchtown to Montgomery

Approximate distance: 7½ miles

Churchtown to Montgomery

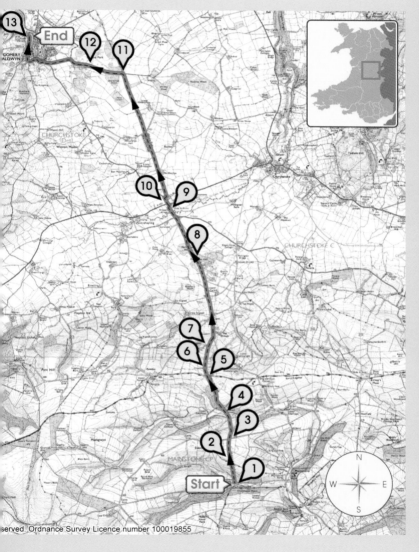

13
End
12
11
GOMERY
ALDWYN
CHURCHSTOKE
10
9
8
CHURCHSTOKE C
7
6
5
4
3
2
1
Start

MAINSTONE CP

N
W   E
S

served. Ordnance Survey Licence number 100019855

Distance: 7½ miles
Map: *OS Explorer Map 216*
Introduction: *A strenuous 7½ mile hike along sections of Offa's Dyke to the historic market town of Montgomery with its impressive Georgian town hall and 13th century castle. The walk has some fairly steep sections but it is well worth the effort as the views are spectacular. The dyke is quite a feat of construction. Offa was king of Mercia from 757 to 796 AD and had a vast kingdom that stretched from the Trent and Mersey rivers in the north to the Thames Valley in the south, and from the Welsh border in the west to the Fens in East Anglia. About 80 miles of the dyke can still be seen along the England-Wales border between the Severn Estuary and the north Wales coast.*
Unlike other walks in this book, this is a linear walk with no easy public transport to get you back to the start. So you will either need two cars or be prepared to pay for a taxi back to your starting point.

Wood carving in Churchtown church

1. Start of the walk – Churchtown: SO 265873

This walk begins outside the quaint old church in Churchtown, where there's a church but no town!

Walk down the road for around 40 yards and turn right, hopping over a stile clearly marked Offa's Dyke footpath.

You're now heading towards the Kerry Ridgeway which is about 1½ miles from here. The ridgeway is an ancient drovers' way that also marks the border between England and Wales in places.

There's no gentle introduction to this walk, just a steep climb up a grassy slope into ancient woods and on to the next stile.

From here you'll get your first glimpse of the dyke as it snakes its way up the hillside above you.

To the left you'll notice a second bank which experts believe may have been built by the Welsh on the other side, but nothing is certain when it comes to the dyke.

Halfway up are badger sets, a common feature along here. It's also a great place to catch your breath and look back over the stunning views and green, sculpted hills.

Offa's Dyke

2. Offa's Dyke: SO 263878

The dyke is a curious feature in the landscape; at times completely obvious and man-made in its appearance but barely distinguishable at other times from the banks and hedgerows running along the field boundaries.

Although the dyke has suffered from erosion, mainly due to man's activities, there are still some steep sections where you can clearly see what an impressive sight it must have been 1,200 years ago.

Follow the path for about 400 yards up to the top of the hill and cross over a stile.

Walk across a rough gravel track to the opposite bank and head up back onto the top of the dyke, skirting colourful fields of crops and wild flowers in summer.

3. Minor road: SO 263883

Walk for ⅓ mile, passing a myriad of patchwork fields and follow a path down towards a minor road.

The views from here are impressive, staring down into the heart of the valley below where the River Unk winds between Nut Wood and Upper Edenhope Hill.

Cross over the stile opposite and head down into the field following the track parallel to the woods, with steeper sections of the dyke to your right **(SO 263883)**.

Continue down a gently-sloping field to the river below and cross over a small wooden footbridge.

4. Wooden footbridge: SO 262888

Turn left and walk up a rough 4x4 track for about 90 yards. Hop over a stile and turn right, following a steep, narrow track skirting Nut Wood.

The track was brimming with life in summer, with ferns and wild flowers lining the path and plenty of warblers and tits in the trees above.

The track levels out at the top. Pass through a kissing gate before arriving in green fields with tall pine trees to your left.

Keep left and walk to the next gate. Along this next section are well-preserved sections of the dyke, which is up to ten feet high in places.

Follow the track to your left – passing a farm pond – and head over another stile onto the Kerry Ridgeway.

5. Kerry Ridgeway: SO 258896

As you stand on the Ridgeway, Shropshire lies behind you and Wales in front.

Cross over the road and stile and follow the sign marked 'Brompton Bridge 2.5 miles' and head down a rough and winding track.

Along this section you'll find badger setts, dug deep into the dyke. The badgers are capable of burrowing straight through the soft earth and often have entrances on either side.

Kerry Ridgeway

6. Views over Shropshire hills: SO 258899

As you round the bend, passing a house named Nyth Brân (Crow's Nest), an incredible vista opens up before you, with magical views over the Shropshire hills.

To the east lies Corndon Hill, Stiperstones and Long Mynd, with Welshpool in the north and the hills of Caeliber Isaf to the west.

If you've got a camera handy, now is the time to use it.

Hop over the wooden stile and follow a steep section of dyke – encased on either side by trees – towards the pretty village of Cwm **(SO 258901)**.

Watch your footing along this stretch as it's littered with badger setts and deep holes.

7. The road to Cwm: SO 260903

Follow the path down past an abandoned quarry hidden away to your left. The track can get quite steep here, before taking you back into fields and eventually leading you out onto a minor road, about ⅓ mile short of Cwm.

Take a few minutes to explore Cwm. There's a lovely old chapel here, Cwm Chapel, which has been converted into a private house.

Follow the signs for 'Brompton 1.5 miles' and you'll shortly arrive at a junction.

Cross over a minor road and follow the dyke path straight on through the woods, taking a short detour to Mellington Hall (sign-posted 'Walkers Welcome').

8. Mellington Hall Hotel: SO 259920

Mellington Hall is now a popular hotel, wedding venue and touring-caravan park.

Follow the woodland path, down some wooden steps towards the back of the house and walk under a stone archway in order to gain a good view of the majestic gothic mansion.

Retrace your steps back into the woods and you'll soon be in open fields, just north of the mansion.

The dyke path runs roughly parallel with the estate road on your right. Head towards a metal gate in the top right hand corner of the field and enter a woodland full of ancient oaks.

Turn left down a shady track lined with pine trees and head towards the estate's gatehouse **(SO 252930)**.

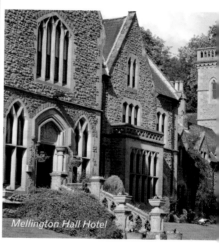
Mellington Hall Hotel

Go on through the imposing iron gates and walk straight onto the B4385, keeping an eye out for any traffic.

Walk along the B4385 for about 450 yards and cross over a stone bridge, marking the border between Shropshire and Powys and of course England and Wales.

9. Remains of a motte and bailey castle: SO 251932

A short distance ahead, on the right hand side of a bend in the road, are the remains of a motte and bailey castle, consisting of a large mound of earth covered with trees (next to Bluebell House).

Originally, there would have been a timber keep on top of the mound, as well as a more substantial dwelling nearby.

field boundary to another wooden stile in the corner of the field.

On the ground lies a stone engraved with the date 1969, although why this was done is unclear.

Hop over the stile and turn left towards Montgomery. The dyke footpath veers to the right here and heads north, all the way to Prestatyn.

12. Montgomery Cricket Club: SO 234963

Follow a metalled road through Lymore Park until you arrive at Montgomery Cricket Club.

This is one of the oldest clubs in Britain, dating back to the 1840s. Famously, the local team once defeated the All England team here by 62 runs, possibly helped by the fact that they fielded 22 players to England's 11!

Beyond the cricket club and impressive duck ponds at Lymore Park, head towards Montgomery, now visible in the distance.

About 450 yards past the duckponds, turn left onto a track which joins up with the B4385 and continue towards Montgomery.

At Montgomery, walk through the town and turn left at the Ivy House Café and head towards the market square, past quirky Georgian and Victorian shops and houses.

10. Blue Bell Hotel and oak tree: SO 250932

Just up the road is the Blue Bell Hotel, an old drovers' pub that has been run by the same family for some 80 years.

Outside is an ancient oak tree, next to two antique petrol pumps (no longer in use), which are well worth a photo.

Carefully cross the busy A489 and after about 50 yards, turn right past Brompton Hall and back onto the dyke path.

Follow the dyke and field boundary for around a mile, with Little Brompton to the west and Rockley to the east.

Cross over a stile and a narrow country lane and head through a wooden gate and into the next set of fields.

11. An engraved stone: SO 241961

Keeping the dyke on your right (which is hard to spot), follow the track for just under a mile along the

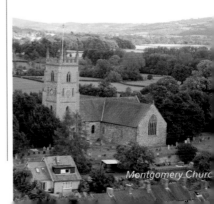

Montgomery Church

Behind the town hall you'll spot the 17th century Dragon Hotel, and beside it, a steep road leading up to the castle perched high above the town.

13. End of the walk – Montgomery Castle: SO 222968

The hike up to the site of Montgomery Castle is steep but definitely worth the effort.

There's not much left of the castle (compared to some of the other castles in Wales) but the panoramic views from the top are sensational.

The castle was built on a strategically -sited plug of volcanic rock on the orders of Henry III in 1223. The town of Montgomery (named after Roger de Montgomerie) soon followed, gaining a Royal Charter in 1227.

Sadly, much of the castle was demolished in 1649 during the Civil War, after Lord Edward Herbert surrendered it to the Parliamentarian forces.

This marks the end of the walk but at least it's downhill back into Montgomery to find your second vehicle or to phone for a local taxi to take you back to your starting point.

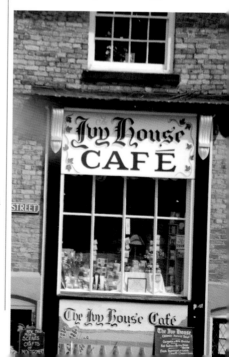

Derek says. . .

THIS IS A LOVELY WALK in Cwm Ratgoed, a secluded valley surrounded by steep forested hillsides just two miles down the road from Corris in Gwynedd.

Everywhere you look in this area, everything is constructed of slate – the walls, roofs, chimneys, steps and fences. The slate was mined here, not quarried, but evidence of the industry still survives on the surface.

The former Ratgoed tramway, built in the 1860s, was once the only route in and out of the valley, and some fine remains of buildings can be seen along the way, including a ruined hamlet and a chapel.

The good thing about this walk is that it packs a lot into a short distance and is fairly flat, making it ideal for families. When I filmed the walk for the TV show, I did it with mums and toddlers and had a picnic on the way. We didn't spot any other walkers en route either, so it's a great place to escape for some peace and quiet.

At the end of the walk, head back into the village and drop into the Corris Institute for a chat, a cuppa and a slice of cake. It also provides shelter from the rain, of which there is plenty in this part of Wales.

7. Cwm Ratgoed

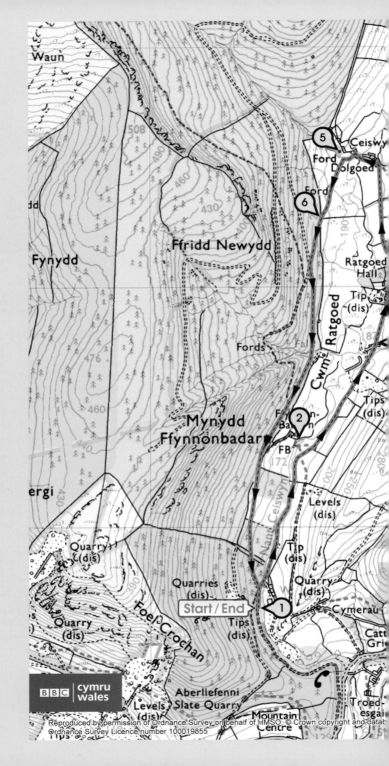

Waun

Fynydd

dd

Fynydd

ergi

Ffridd Newydd

Mynydd
Ffynnonbadarn

Quarry
(dis)

Quarry
(dis)

Foel Crochan

Quarries
(dis)

Start / End 1

Tips
(dis)

Levels
(dis)

Aberllefenni
Slate Quarry

Mountain
Centre

5 Ceisw
Ford
Dolgoed

6 Ford

Ratgoed
Hall

Tip
(dis)

Fords

2

FB
72

Levels
(dis)

Tip
(dis)

Quarry
(dis)

Cymerau

Catt
Gri

Troed-
esgai

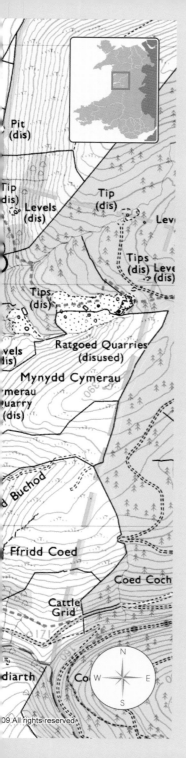

Cwm Ratgoed

Approximate distance: 2½ miles

Pit
(dis)

Tip
(dis)

Tip
(dis)

Levels
(dis)

Leve

Tips
(dis) Leve
(dis)

Tips
(dis)

vels
is)

Ratgoed Quarries
(disused)

Mynydd Cymerau

merau
uarry
(dis)

Buchod

Ffridd Coed

Coed Coch

Cattle
Grid

diarth

Co

Great Welsh Walks

Distance: 2½ miles

Map: *OS Explorer Map OL23*

Introduction: *An easy 2½ mile circular walk through Cwm Ratgoed, a beautiful, sheltered valley just north of Aberllefenni near Corris in Gwynedd. It's a little off the beaten track but is suitable for kids. However the second half of the walk is not suitable for buggies – you can simply retrace your steps from the valley end, and still get a feel for this special place.*

Ffynnon Badarn

locally as Cadbury House, a simple whitewashed stone cottage bought by the Cadbury chocolate family in the 1960s.

The family were very socially aware for the time and allowed staff to use the accommodation for holidays. It was also used by the Bournville family who came here to hill walk.

Ffynnon Badarn – St Padarn's Well – one of the holy wells of Wales, is said to be located nearby. Its exact location is unknown but it's believed to be located somewhere in the woods beyond the house.

Walk through a small wooded area, past an old slate wall on your right. You'll soon pass another slate tip and a farm gate before crossing a river in order to arrive at some derelict buildings.

1. Start of the walk: SH 775108

Park your car in the lay-by on the right hand side of the road **(SH 774107)** and walk up the road. Turn right, cross over a bridge and head along a rough 4x4 track alongside the farm.

Pass through a metal gate and continue along the track, keeping the river and marshy area to your left for about ⅓ mile, until you arrive at the first slate tip **(SH 776112)**.

Above you are rolling hills. Sycamore, rowan, oak and ash trees can all be found growing along the river bank.

2. Ffynnon Badarn: SH 777113

From here you'll catch your first glimpse of the building known

3. Old quarry shop: SH 779118

At one time there were four buildings here which housed the local quarry workers. The end building, closest to the tramway, doubled up as the local shop and had a bay window, allowing customers to peer inside.

A little further on, buried amongst the trees, is a former Calvinistic Methodist chapel which opened in 1871.

Remains of the chapel

Head up the lane. To your left, below the track, are the old stables. In 1936 the nearby quarry reservoir burst its banks and the water cascaded down the hillside, smashing into the stables and nearly killing the family who worked there.

Miraculously, everyone survived the incident and the stream continues to run through the decaying buildings.

It's only a small building, made completely of slate with ornate arches and doorway. Worshippers would have had to travel long distances to get to what is still an isolated spot.

Beyond the chapel, continue up the track until you reach a fork in the road. Keep left and walk towards a large oak tree shading a ruined slate building, which was once the blacksmith's shop. Behind it are the old slate dressing sheds.

Ahead, on your left, is a clearing and a pleasant picnic area – the top of which was once a slate tip, now grassed over.

On a clear day there are some lovely views down over the green valley you've just walked up.

Beyond the old stables is a small hut once used to weigh the slate. Opposite, amongst the moss and ferns, is the incline running up the hillside where slate wagons ran.

4. Ratgoed Hall: SH 780121

Around the corner, you'll arrive at an impressive walled driveway leading to Ratgoed Hall. At one time this would have had a much grander entrance in the form of a gate and bridge.

The hall was built around 1870 by Horatio Nelson Hughes, a wealthy Liverpudlian quarry owner.

In the early 1940s the hall became a youth hostel, popular with army servicemen based at Tonfannau Camp near Tywyn who used to go hill walking when off duty.

Ratgoed Hall

The Welsh word Ratgoed translates as 'wooded hillside' and suggests that the deciduous woodland on the hillside to the right was once more abundant.

Pass through a metal farm gate and out into open countryside. The land here offers marshy grazing for sheep, with a muddy 4x4 track running through the middle.

Cross over a couple of shallow streams, stopping at a large sycamore tree on your left, just before a metal farm gate. Beyond the gate is Dolgoed, an ancient Quaker home, said to be the oldest house in Meirionnydd and privately owned by the same family since the 1600s.

The Quakers who lived here would have walked miles over the mountains in order to worship in Tabor, near Dolgellau.

A number of leading industrialists in the 19th century were Quakers, including the Rowntree, Cadbury and Clark families to whom the industrial revolution owed much.

At the sycamore tree turn left and walk across a grassy field, past the solar panels, towards the fence line and stile opposite.

Climb over the stile and carefully descend a steep, uneven track that leads down to some large Douglas fir trees.

Turn right and make your way towards a slippery wooden bridge. Cross over and walk on through a metal gate and into a field. Keep left.

Ceiswyn farmhouse

Pass under a beech tree and cross over a small slate footbridge spanning Nant Ceiswyn, which flows down from Mynydd Ceiswyn to the north.

5. Ceiswyn farmhouse: SH 778126

The river gives its name to this 16th century farmhouse which has an interesting history.

The Red Brigands of Dinas Mawddwy were an infamous group of red-haired highwaymen who operated in this lawless area during the 16th century.

They achieved notoriety after capturing and killing a local judge, Sir Lewis Owain, in a revenge attack for having some of their members tried and executed.

The judge's companion at the time was a Siôn Lloyd who survived the ambush and lived in this house. Legend has it that Lloyd hid swords in the chimney in case of future attacks.

6. End of the walk – forestry track: SH 777123

Cross the stream and follow the track to the left leading up into the pine forest until you arrive at a private forestry road.

Keep left and enjoy the quiet woods and sounds of the river to your left, catching occasional glimpses of the other side of the valley that you walked along earlier.

Colourful mosses and lichen line the track along with fabulous wild flowers in summer, such as foxgloves, heather and gorse. In amongst the trees you'll spot remains of the slate industry in the shape of old huts and mine workings.

Pass through the last kissing gate, and head on down the hill along a meandering track to the starting point at the bridge and the end of the walk.

Track from Ceiswyn farmhouse to pine forest

Derek says. . .

GARTH MOUNTAIN, known locally as 'the Garth', was the inspiration for the book and film, *The Englishman Who Went Up a Hill but Came Down a Mountain*, starring Hugh Grant.

The Garth lies just north of Cardiff. It may be only 307 metres (1,007 feet) high but it's worth the climb. From the summit there are panoramic views. When it's clear, you can see the Brecon Beacons to the north and right across the Bristol Channel to Somerset towards the south. You can also make out Castell Coch and the Millennium Stadium.

The Coed y Bedw nature reserve run by the local Wildlife Trust is a hidden gem. It's hard to believe you're so close to a busy road as you wander through ancient woodlands of ash, birch and oak trees. There's plenty of bird and wildlife here too, along with rare plants. In spring, there are carpets of snowdrops and bluebells.

This short walk is ideal for escaping the big city and en route you also pass a lovely pub, the Gwaelod y Garth Inn, where you can stop for refreshments or a bowl of soup.

I filmed this walk for the television programme in the company of members of Welsh Women Walking, a friendly bunch of ladies, who raise money for charity.

8. Garth Mountain

Approximate distance: 4½ miles

Garth Mountain

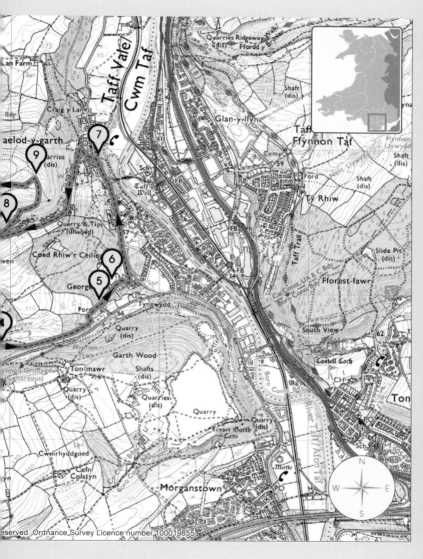

Great Welsh Walks

Distance: 4½ miles
Map: *OS Explorer Map 151*
Introduction: *A fairly strenuous 4½ mile circular walk to the summit of Garth Mountain. The walk begins in Pentyrch, north of Cardiff, and takes you down through Coed y Bedw nature reserve, into the quaint village of Gwaelod y Garth. It's then a steep climb up to the summit of Garth Mountain before heading back down into Pentyrch. Despite being so close to civilisation, it's an area rich in folklore and tales of mysterious goings-on.*

1. Start of the walk – Lewis Arms, Pentyrch: ST 101822

From the pub, walk along Heol Goch and turn right onto Cefn Bychan lane.

After about 500 yards, turn left at the signpost and follow a short, steep trail down through woods to the road **(ST 106823)**.

Take care crossing the road. Opposite, you'll find a field with a wooden stile. Climb over and follow a muddy track leading downhill towards a large metal gate.

2. Track down the hill: ST 105824

Along the way you'll pass through beautiful meadows, full of wild flowers and ancient trees some of which are 600 years old. Garth Mountain lies ahead of you in the distance.

Pass some large drainage pipes on the grass and head through the gate **(ST 106826)**. Follow the track to the next gate and turn right. Follow the hedge line along to a stile that takes you into the nature reserve.

3. Coed y Bedw Nature Reserve: ST 107826

The reserve is owned and managed by the local Wildlife Trust and it's hard to believe you're so close to a busy main road as you make your way down through the ancient, broadleaved woodlands of oak, birch and ash trees.

The pathways can get very muddy, especially after rain, so take your time crossing over the streams and wooden bridges.

There is plenty of wildlife here and the woods are alive with the sounds of tits and warblers in spring.

4. Morgan Thomas's ruined cottage: ST 108826

A short way into the reserve, you'll stumble across a ruined cottage belonging to former mine-owner and poet, Morgan Thomas, who lived here 100 years ago.

Iron ore was once mined here but the tramways that used to cart away the ore, coal and charcoal are now overgrown with mosses and wild flowers.

Myths and legends have grown up around this valley. The water bubbling up from Ffynnon Gruffydd

Morgan Thomas's ruined cottage

is said to have healing properties and fairies supposedly dance here on Hallowe'en!

There are ghosts too. Y Brenin Llwyd (King of the Mist) haunts the old mine and there's also a one-armed ghost of a man who apparently committed suicide at the cottage in 1930.

Continue along uneven tracks, taking care as you go. But don't forget to look up too, as you'll pass by some magnificent old trees.

As you near the edge of the reserve, head down a steeper section of path towards a large wooden boardwalk and bridge crossing over a stream, passing a wildlife information board and gate.

The walk suddenly opens up now, with grassy meadows to your left and a babbling stream and moss-covered rocks to your right.

Look out for a cleverly made seat, carved into a tree branch on your left. Keep left and follow the track through a gate and into a dense pine forest.

5. Pine forest: ST 116830

Unlike a lot of planted pine forests, this one is actually alive with birds and has a surprising amount of light flooding through the canopy to the forest floor.

After a short distance, you emerge on the far side of the woods in the picturesque hamlet of Georgetown.

6. Georgetown: ST 117830

Walk through a wooden gate, past colourful terraced houses and head downhill from Georgetown. Turn left and walk straight up into Gwaelod y Garth village.

In Elizabethan times, Gwaelod y Garth was known for its iron-ore mines but these days this sleepy village is part of the Cardiff commuter belt.

7. Gwaelod y Garth: ST 116839

Just before the Gwaelod y Garth Inn, turn left and walk up a steep tarmac road **(ST 116839)**.

You'll find the route begins to get a little more strenuous from here on in.

At the hairpin bend in the road, keep left and head onwards and upwards, for around ½ mile towards viewpoints at the top.

Entrance to pine forest

As the road levels out, you'll pass above an old barn on your left, which is busy with visiting swallows in summer. Below it is the pine forest you walked through earlier.

8. Garth Mountain track: ST 109834

Follow the waymarker sign on your right and head up a steep hillside track towards the mountain top. During summer, the hillsides are covered in bracken and there are sweeping views all the way up.

As the track levels out, you'll get your first glimpse of Cardiff in the distance with the Bristol Channel beyond.

9. False summit: ST 112838

The final leg-burning push leads you up a steep grassy track towards a false summit – the actual summit is a little further on!

Once you reach the top of this plateau you'll have panoramic views over the world below, with views over Taffs Well, the Taff valley, Cardiff with its iconic landmarks, and Somerset in the distance.

To the west you may be able to make out Aberthaw Power Station and to the north, the Brecon Beacons. To the east lie the towers of the Severn Bridge.

New bracken growth

It can get pretty windy up here, so be prepared as you make your way along the final leg to the real summit of Garth Mountain, standing at a height of 1,007 feet.

There are a couple of paths leading to the summit but the most direct one heads towards the trig point atop one of four Bronze Age burial mounds which have stood here for 4,000 years.

10. Burial mound and summit: ST 103835

The early to middle Bronze Age round barrows here date from around 2000 BC and are scheduled ancient historic monuments. We can only wonder about the significance of this site in ancient times.

11. End of the walk – back to the Lewis Arms

From the summit, head south **(ST 103832)** down the mountain and cross over the minor road (which you turned off earlier on your way up).

At the junction **(ST 099829)**, keep left and head straight down Mountain Road back into Pentyrch and the Lewis Arms where the walk began.

Garth Hill burial mound and summit

Views across Cardiff to the Bristol Channel and north Devon

Derek says. . .

THE HAFOD ESTATE in Cwm Ystwyth dates back to the Georgian era and is one of the finest examples of a 'picturesque' landscape, with its lush woodlands, gorges and waterfalls.

What I like most about this walk is that it's full of surprises with hidden attractions like the Cavern Cascade. The Allt Dihanog tunnel is another exciting feature, with lovely views when you come out at the other end. If you're lucky you may see birds of prey, such as the magnificent red kite.

You may find the walk hard going at times but there are alternative paths if you prefer something easier or just fancy a picnic by the river followed by a short stroll. Rainfall in the area is high with more than 1,800mm (71 inches) a year, so bring your waterproofs if the weather is not set fair.

Hafod was a 'must see' destination for the early tourist visiting Wales back in the 18th century. If Thomas Johnes, its creator, was around today I am sure he would be delighted to know that it is still attracting visitors.

Devil's Bridge is just down the road too, so why not combine your walk with a trip on the Vale of Rheidol steam railway.

9. Hafod Estate

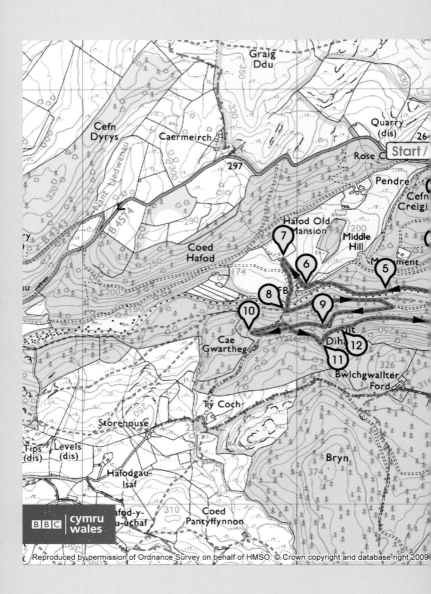

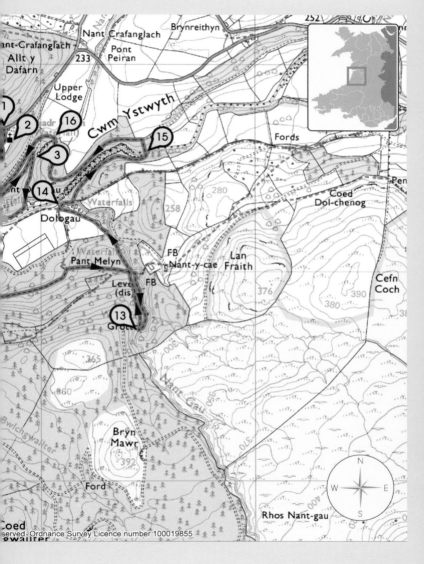

Distance: 5½ miles

Map: *OS Explorer Map 213*

Introduction: *A moderate 5½ mile circular walk around the Hafod Estate in the Ystwyth valley, near Devil's Bridge. It's a relatively strenuous walk, passing through woodlands, gorges and within sight of spectacular waterfalls. The walk combines elements of several different waymarked routes but is well signposted throughout. Along the way you'll visit the key manmade features at Hafod, one of the most influential 'picturesque' landscapes of the late 18th century anywhere in Europe. Dogs are allowed but must be kept under control, especially near livestock.*

1. Start of the walk – Hafod car park: SN 768737

The walk begins in the car park just off the B4574, near Hafod Church. The first section of the walk follows the original Lady's Walk, marked as a blue route on the Hafod Estate map.

Walk down a well-marked trail through the woods and on to the back gate of the churchyard on your left.

The wall here is covered with moss and ferns, and gives you a good idea of what lies ahead in this watery landscape of gorges and waterfalls.

Old family gravestone at Hafod Church

2. Hafod Church: SN 769736

Built by Thomas Johnes in 1801, it was ravaged by fire in 1932 when most of its contents was destroyed or damaged, including a beautifully carved, commemorative marble statue to Johnes's daughter, Mariamné, sculpted by Sir Francis Chantrey.

Make your way down a winding trail through open pine forests, following the blue waymarked route.

At the bottom of the track you'll join an old estate road. Cross over the road and follow the blue route towards the spectacular Peiran Falls.

3. Peiran Falls: SN 770736

The waterfall here was once spanned by Pont Newydd, a stone and timber bridge, which carried Johnes's carriage driveway over the gorge. It no longer exists but you can still see the stone abutments on each side, which you'll walk past later.

The ground here drops steeply in two main stages, creating a smaller upper fall and a larger lower one.

A surprising volume of water flows down through this steep, narrow gorge but it's best viewed after a decent downpour. In very wet weather the lower fall forms

Rustic rails

Peiran Falls

a double cascade either side of a pointed rock.

The Peiran valley is steep-sided, with rocky, lower slopes covered in moss, ferns, scattered stunted oaks and rhododendrons.

Follow the path down the right bank. In a few yards, you'll come to some old stonework on either side of the path known as the Rustic Alcove **(SN 770735)**.

These old stone walls are all that remain of a summer-house or covered seat that once stood here. Johnes actually deliberately built it

across the path, to obscure the view of the Peiran Falls as visitors made their way up the path.

On entering the building, the view was suddenly revealed, adding a wow factor to this picturesque scene.

To your left, Nant Peiran tumbles down a rocky channel in numerous small cascades, rapids and pools.

Shortly beyond the point where your path crosses a track, the stream makes another pretty cascade before joining the River Ystwyth.

The walk curves right, following the river bank and continues through a coniferous and deciduous woodland, where you can enjoy the open sections of the river with its large pebbles and boulders.

To help you feel secure, there are a few handrails along this stretch of path. One is made entirely from tree branches and it is these quirky elements which make this walk so enjoyable.

Just beyond a bend in the river, a small path branches right and crosses a forestry road to arrive at Mrs Johnes's flower garden which has lain derelict for many years.

4. Mrs Johnes's Garden: SN 767731

The garden is roughly a triangular-shaped acre of land, surrounded by a large dry stone wall with stone arches on both the east and west sides of the garden.

Created in about 1786, it was influenced by William Mason's vision of paradise in his poem 'The English Garden'.

The Hafod Trust aims to replant the garden with species of trees and shrubs that were available at that time, including recently introduced 'exotic' American plants.

Leave the garden, retrace your steps to the blue trail (Lady's Walk) and follow the river until you arrive at a modern bridge and forestry road.

Walk straight past the bridge and head south, keeping the river on your left until you arrive at a wide bend in the river. There's a tranquil picnic spot here and plenty of perfectly formed pebbles with which to practise skimming.

5. Following the River Ystwyth

The landscape opens up nicely along this next section with wild flowers and heather lining the river banks and a grazed field to your right.

In Johnes's time this was an important open space at the heart of the estate. To restore his vision of a varied landscape, it has been returned to grassland by the Forestry Commission after several decades under conifers. A few Highland cattle have been introduced here to manage the habitat.

Less than ½ mile away, at the end of the field **(SN 763731)**, veer right and head up a steep track through fir trees until you arrive at one of the estate drives.

6. Viewpoint over the river: SN 761730

Turn left and follow the drive for a few yards, stopping at a viewpoint and seating area overlooking the River Ystwyth.

Continue along the drive, crossing a cattle grid before turning right towards the remains of Thomas Johnes's mansion and the Hafod Estate offices (old stables).

Following the River Ystwyth

7. The Hafod mansion: SN 759732

During Johnes's time the mansion consisted of a two-storey, Gothic-style building. It later formed the south-east wing of a much larger house that included stables, offices, an octagonal library and 160 foot long conservatory.

The house experienced its fair share of fires, demolitions and additions as it changed hands over the years but it gradually became neglected.

It was demolished in 1958, but the Victorian stable block was retained, along with some surrounding walls. A fountain has been reinstated in one of these walls.

Retrace your steps back to the road again and turn right after the rock-cutting, and then left down a grassy track.

8. Alpine bridge: SN 760730

About 100 yards to the south is a wooden, alpine bridge taking you over the river.

Just before the bridge a trail leads towards what initially looks like an old wall but is, in fact, a building.

The floor of this cylindrical building lies about 20 feet below ground level and was originally used as an ice store for the mansion house.

Return to the path and cross over the bridge and turn left, following red waymarker signs along a broad path that follows the Gentleman's Walk uphill.

After crossing over, see if you can spot a tree on the hillside above you, to your right.

I thought the tree bore an uncanny resemblance to a Tree Ent from the

The 'whistling' tree

book, *Lord of the Rings* – complete with whistling mouth, nose and eyes.

Follow a zigzagging trail through a dark wood, emerging at a crossroads. Go straight ahead, following the red marker-posts down a narrow path, with a stream below you.

9. Rustic Bridge: SN 761729

You'll soon arrive at a fairytale, wooden bridge – known as the Rustic Bridge – which lies in the rock-strewn Bwlchgwallter valley, full of small cascading waterfalls and green mosses that carpet the ground and trees.

Upstream of the bridge is a fine waterfall, and above it an arched bridge, which you'll walk over later as you head uphill on a forestry road.

Carefully cross the wooden bridge and head up some steep wooden steps and into the woods beyond.

As you ascend, you'll be rewarded occasionally with glimpses of the river bed, far below.

The habitat changes dramatically up here, with moss carpeting the trees and ground, and looks completely different to anything you've experienced on the walk so far.

You'll eventually exit the woods and, after crossing the bridge you saw earlier from the Rustic Bridge, turn right onto a forestry road, briefly leaving the Gentleman's Walk.

Continue uphill, and head towards a viewpoint beyond a conifer plantation. The trail is marked with a red waymarker.

10. Viewpoint: SN 758728

Follow a short track to your right, up a small hill to a spot with sweeping views to the west over the river valley and the mansion fields.

Retrace your footsteps back down the road and then branch right, following the red marker signs along a mossy path into a dark conifer plantation.

11. Mossy Seat Falls: SN 761728

Soon you'll arrive back at the steep, picturesque Bwlchgwallter valley where the stream descends in a series of falls, torrents and pools.

Be aware that the next section of path, including the bridge and steps, can be slippery, especially after rainfall. The whole area here is very damp and, as the name suggests, mossy.

Standing on the narrow wooden bridge, you'll be rewarded with great views of the waterfalls gushing down the gorge.

There was once a seat here on a mossy island situated between two branches of the stream, but a few stone slabs are all that remain of it.

Take care on the next stretch of path, which runs along a rock-cut shelf. The route then turns away from the stream, crosses an old extraction track, and follows a red waymarker towards the Allt Dihanog tunnel.

View from trail above Allt Dihanog tunnel

12. Allt Dihanog tunnel: SN 763729

The tunnel is another exciting feature on this walk and leads the path through an otherwise impassable bluff of rock.

Head through the tunnel until you reach daylight on the other side. The next section of walk requires concentration – there are steps, uneven ground and steep drops.

But there are also viewpoints from which you can enjoy fine vistas over the treetops to the far side of the Ystwyth valley.

Beyond the viewpoints, the conifer woods close in and there is a long section of path with little to see, until you reach the estate's ancient beech woods.

The Hafod beech trees are arranged in several clumps with a few huge specimens believed to be more than 200 years old.

Eventually you emerge onto a track at Pant Melyn, with a beech-covered hill in front of you. There are two waymarked routes over and round the summit. Turn right and follow the main track.

Ignore any turnings right or left and keep straight on until you reach a steep descent towards a stream and the Nant Gau valley.

Do not cross the stream by way of the footbridge, but head right on a narrow ascending path.

You are now on a public right-of-way, which happens to be a dead end. It is also the Gentleman's Walk, so continue to follow the red waymarkers to the Cavern Cascade.

You'll pass numerous waterfalls as you make your way up this steep narrow valley.

On one of the bends next to the path, and to your right, you'll pass what is probably an early exploratory mining level. Do not go into it; a more exciting cave is just a short distance away.

13. Cavern Cascade: SN 775727

The path approaches a rocky bluff, behind which the stream runs into a deep, narrow, rock-cut channel.

To the right, you'll find a sizeable tunnel cut into the rock, reached by carefully clambering up a rocky slope. Take care also on the flat rocks in front of the tunnel.

Cavern Cascade

The rock-cut tunnel runs straight and then turns slightly to the left, towards its far end.

You'll hear the waterfall before you see it but nothing prepares you for what comes next.

Rounding the bend, you'll be greeted by a torrent of water pouring down over the end of the tunnel and into a deep pool below.

Retrace your footsteps back to the beech trees at Pant Melyn. Take care as you exit the tunnel.

Follow a path to the right that passes through a gap in a stone wall and then follow the red waymarkers alongside Nant Gau, where there are more cascades and rock features to enjoy.

At the bottom of the wood, a stile leads you into an open field. Follow the track down along the eastern edge of the field towards another stile.

Beyond the stile, turn right down the track and walk towards Dologau Bridge.

14. Dologau Bridge: SN 771733

This lovely, stone-arched bridge across the Ystwyth was built by Thomas Johnes in about 1790.

Do not cross the bridge, but turn right at a green waymarker (Ystwyth Gorge walk) and head through a small gate and onto a wooden footbridge.

It's now a pleasant hike up through the woods above the river and dramatic gorges below. The river runs westwards, dropping down a deeply cut, narrow gorge. Eventually you come to two stone pillars beside the path.

This was once the Gothic Arcade **(SN 774736)** – an ornamental

Chain bridge

viewpoint with four columns and three arches covering a seating area.

It's a great spot to stop and admire the view, including an unusual footbridge spanning a photogenic gorge below.

15. Chain bridge

A short walk brings you down to the wonderfully wobbly 'chain bridge', placed here in 1805.

It was originally supported by chains, later replaced by cables. By the middle of the 20th century only the cast-iron pillars remained, but it was restored in 2003.

Cross over the bridge and head up into the woods. Follow the trail until the woods give way to farmland. Take in the scenery, curious rock formations and gorges sculpted by the unrelenting flow of water.

Once across the farmland, you're on the homeward leg of the walk, climbing steeply up into the woods and following the green trail high above the river opposite.

16. Remains of Pont Newydd: SN 771736

A wide track, formerly the Cwmystwyth drive, built by Johnes in 1813–14, leads through a quiet, coniferous woodland. Arriving at the Peiran valley, you will see the remains of Pont Newydd that once spanned the Peiran Falls.

Your route crosses the River Peiran by means of a narrow wooden footbridge, a short way upstream. This is the site of an ancient flour mill, but no building survives.

17. End of the walk – back up to the car park

Rejoin the old carriage drive and follow it to the right. Soon, the green route is joined by the blue route, ascending from the foot of the Peiran Falls.

Follow the blue waymarkers up to the main drive, which you cross.

The path then takes you back up to your starting point, passing Hafod Church before arriving back at the car park.

Derek says. . .

HOLY ISLAND, the last stop before Ireland, offers some of the best walking on Anglesey. And this walk won't disappoint.

The rocky and rugged path takes you along the coast and up and around Holyhead Mountain. It is only 220 metres (722 feet) high but Mynydd Twr (as it's called in Welsh) feels like a proper mountain, with steep drops to the north and west.

On reaching the summit, you are rewarded with fine views of Holyhead harbour and across Anglesey to Snowdonia. On a clear day see if you can spot the Isle of Man and the Wicklow Mountains in Ireland.

The Iron Age hillfort of Caer y Twr is one of the best preserved ancient settlements in Wales, whilst the coastline is famous worldwide for its bird and marine life, its beauty and maritime history.

The views from South Stack and North Stack are amazing, and there is no shortage of seabirds. Every summer 4,000 visit the area, including guillemots, razorbills and puffins. For more information, pop into the RSPB visitor centre inside Ellin's Tower where there are binoculars and a telescope available.

At Breakwater Country Park, look out for the stonechats, choughs and peregrine falcons along with oystercatchers and cormorants on the coast. And you may even spot a seal or two.

Approximate distance: 5 miles

84

Fog Signal
Station

Caves

North Stack /
Ynys Arw

Parliament House

Caves

Gogarth Bay

Holyhead Mounta
Mynydd Tw

83

MH & MLW

Holyhead Br
Parc Gwled

Radio
Stations

South Stack /
Ynys Lawd

Foel   Resr
Qu

FB   Cerydd

Cytiau'r Gwyddelod
(settlement)

Tan-y-cytiau

82 Ellin's
Tower

Plas
Nicol

Ty'n-nant

Ty-mawr

Holyhead

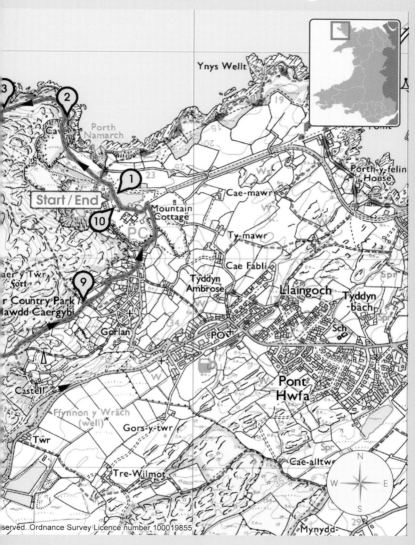

Distance: 5 miles

Map: *OS Explorer Map 262*

Introduction: *This 5 mile circular walk begins at the Breakwater Country Park at Holyhead, taking in North Stack, Holyhead Mountain, South Stack and Ellin's Tower.*

Part of this walk is on The Isle of Anglesey Coastal Path – a 125 mile long route which runs through some of the grandest coastal scenery in Wales, with wide sandy bays and estuaries, intimate coves, dramatic cliffs, sand dunes and forests.

The coastline of Anglesey has been designated as one of Wales's five official Areas of Outstanding Natural Beauty. Birdwatchers flock here to see the visiting seabirds in summer.

Breakwater Country Park

1. Start of the walk – Breakwater Country Park, SH 226833

Walk out of the park past a large man-made pond and you'll quickly join up with the coastal trail. Head through a wooden gate towards the cliffs, where you'll notice large rock slides on the quarry face.

At one time there were eleven quarrying sites at the Breakwater Quarries and stone from here (seven million tonnes) was used to build the famous Holyhead Breakwater which was completed in 1873, making it the largest in Europe.

Walk through the now disused quarry for about 150 yards and head up some rock steps carved out of the hillside and up onto the Isle of Anglesey Coastal Path.

2. Views over the breakwater: SH 223838

Behind you are views over Holyhead harbour, two picturesque little bays below and the north-west coast of Anglesey in the distance.

Along this stretch, as you follow a rocky track towards North Stack, you'll spot ferry boats regularly zipping in and out of the harbour en route to Ireland.

The path here is very uneven, made up of scattered rocks lined with gorse, heather and a sprinkling of common and spotted orchids.

Be careful as you tread the rocky

Views over the breakwater

path but don't forget to look around at the views, as you might spot the odd porpoise in the turquoise-blue water below.

Magazine hut

3. Magazine hut: SH 221837

Head up the hill past an old stone hut, once used by the quarry to store explosives and dynamite.

Continue past the magazine hut and along a steepening path. You will come to Trinity House, the ornate stone building that was also used to store gunpowder for a large cannon that was once positioned on the clifftop.

The canon would fire warning shots to any passing ships venturing too close to the rocks but it eventually fell into the sea. It has since been

recovered and is now on show at the Breakwater Country Park.

4. North Stack foghorn station: SH 216840

Keep right and stay on the winding coastal path until you arrive at North Stack foghorn station, now redundant but home to local artist Philippa Jacobs when we visited.

The views from North Stack are staggering. Here you are surrounded by steep sea cliffs with seals and porpoises below, seabirds above, and rock climbers somewhere in between!

Directly beneath the stack is an enormous sea cave and inaccessible small beach where grey seals give birth to their pups in the autumn.

You'll often see climbers dangling from ropes along the steep cliffs hereabouts but be extremely careful where you walk as the drops are sheer. And you definitely need to keep an eye on your children and dogs.

From here there are sweeping views over to nearby South Stack with its towering sea cliffs surrounded by wide expanses of blue sea. You can see why an artist would choose to live here.

The light is constantly changing with every passing weather front but it must be a frightening spot to be perched on during violent winter storms.

From here, head south along the coastal footpath towards Holyhead

North Stack foghorn station

Mountain, passing a ruined telegraph station (**SH 217834**) now reclaimed by nature.

The telegraph station was built by the Trustees of Liverpool Docks in 1827 and was the most westerly station along the north Wales coast. A ship could semaphore to the station and a message warning of its arrival could be passed on to Holyhead Port and then to Liverpool. A signal from here could be conveyed along the line in as little as 23 seconds.

Heading downhill now, you'll spot a winding trail taking you off to the left and then up a steep, indistinct rocky track towards the 220 metre high summit of Mynydd Tŵr (Holyhead Mountain) and the Iron Age hillfort of Caer y Tŵr.

5. Caer y Tŵr hillfort: SH 218829

The fort's defensive walls are made up of naturally occurring, rocky outcrops as well as quite extensive stone ramparts to the north and east of this seven hectare site (approximately three football pitches in size).

The fort was probably occupied

Looking back towards North Stack foghorn station

before Roman times and the conquering Romans continued to use the site to keep an eye on Irish Sea raiders. You can still find remains of the watch-tower they built on the summit.

Opposite the fort, on a ridge overlooking Gogarth Bay, is a small, Bronze Age burial cairn **(SH 214828)**.

Once you reach the trig point, you'll be rewarded with 360-degree views over Holyhead harbour, the Carneddau mountains, and Snowdon in the distance.

From the top, wander down southwards across a rocky landscape and onto a wide path leading to South Stack and Ellin's Tower.

Keep an eye out for the rare spotted-rock rose that clings to the dry, rocky areas, hidden within the scrub along the sides of the path.

This tiny plant, with yellow and crimson-spotted petals, only flowers once in its lifetime and drops its petals within a few hours, making it extremely difficult to find.

Another species endemic to South Stack is the *spatulate fleawort*, found here and nowhere else in the world!

Spotted rock rose

6. Views over South Stack: SH 206823

Follow the path, until you come to a ruined building, which on a wet and windy day would provide excellent shelter. It looks over South Stack lighthouse.

The 91 foot tall lighthouse has been warning ships of danger since 1809 and the cliffs above it are a great place to admire the pink sea thrift and watch the seabirds down below.

From up here you'll see choughs, various gulls, the odd puffin and peregrine, thousands of guillemots and razorbills and even the occasional porpoise.

View towards the burial cairn

South Stack lighthouse

Ellin's Tower

The tower is actually a Victorian folly, built in 1868 as a summerhouse by the Lord Lieutenant of Anglesey for his wife, Ellin Williams.

The RSPB have telescopes for you to use along with a remote-controlled video camera to help pinpoint the elusive puffins, so pop in and have a look. Entry is free.

You can also watch nesting choughs, tucked under the cliff, thanks to a video camera which streams live footage onto a giant plasma screen inside the tower.

Leaving the tower, head back up the steps and across the road you walked down earlier.

8. Mountain track: SH 207822

Follow a track leading up behind the small car park above Ellin's Tower and back towards the mountain and a concrete path in the distance.

Head north-east as it skirts around the base of Holyhead Mountain **(SH 218826)** taking you past its southern end.

9. Medieval field boundaries: SH 224827

The track runs almost parallel to South Stack Road, which is an alternative route. Head into the fields, where you'll encounter

To your right are nice views down over North Stack and the Skerries further out to sea in the distance.

You might also recognise the rocks below the bridge at South Stack. It was here that the Roxy Music album cover for *Siren* was photographed, featuring Jerry Hall as a mermaid draped over jagged rocks, with Ellin's Tower in the background. Continue along the coast towards Ellin's Tower.

7. Ellin's Tower: SH 206820

The tower is easily accessible and one of the few places in Wales where you can literally park your car, have a bite to eat and walk just a few hundred yards and see thousands of visiting seabirds such as guillemots, puffins, choughs, fulmars, razorbills and gannets.

Track down from the mountain

medieval field boundaries, and follow the track between some old dry stone walls.

10. End of the walk – road back to Breakwater Country Park: SH 227830

Follow the stone walls and, at a crossroads in the paths, walk straight across until you reach a lane.

Turn left by the houses and left again at the T-junction and walk to the end of the lane.

The path then bears left, then right, following a fenced path. Walk down a set of steps and you will find yourself back at the Country Park.

Views towards Snowdonia from the mountain

Derek says. . .

MY COUSIN and his family live in Bagillt, so it was nice to visit the area again and film a walk in this corner of Wales. Flintshire is better known for its industry than its wildlife and history, but there's plenty of that here too, including a magnificent castle and the ruins of an abbey.

The Greenfield valley is a hidden gem and make sure you visit St Winifride's holy well, one of the seven wonders of Wales, where you can pray for fine weather and bathe in the healing waters, as I did. Although be warned – it's freezing!

The Flintshire coast is one of the newer stretches of the Wales Coast Path, with wonderful views across the Dee estuary. It is also great for birdwatching; if you're lucky, you might spot little egrets and spoonbills.

This is a varied walk in a relatively dry part of Wales with an annual rainfall of less than 1,000mm (36 inches). Flintshire is also home to the hottest place in Wales. At Hawarden Bridge, 35.2 Celsius (95.4 Fahrenheit) was recorded in August 1990.

Another good thing about this walk is that it is fairly flat, and there is also a regular bus service back to the start.

11. Holywell to Flint Castle

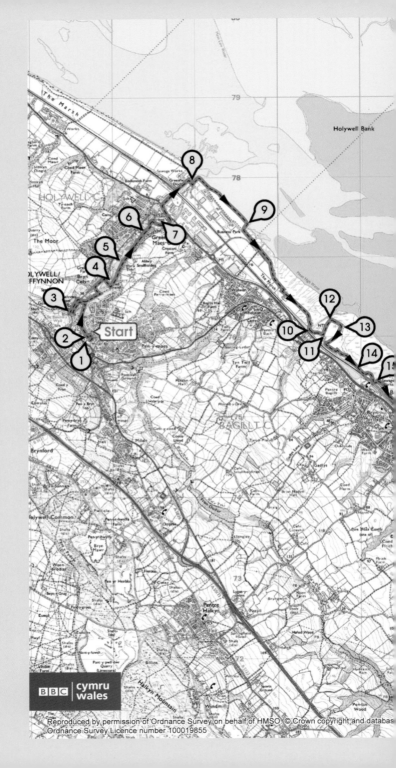

Holywell
to Flint Castle

Approximate distance: 8 miles

Great Welsh Walks

Distance: 8 miles
Map: *OS Explorer Map: 265*
Introduction: *This moderate, 8 mile linear walk begins in Holywell. From the town centre you'll head down through Greenfield Valley Heritage Park with its fascinating history of industry powered by the local streams. Along the way you'll visit St Winefride's Well, the Welsh equivalent of Lourdes, before heading back into the valley, leaving the woods at the romantic ruins of Basingwerk Abbey. It's then a short walk to Greenfield Docks on the banks of the Dee estuary, with fabulous views over the salt marshes and Wirral as you weave in and out of inlets and old docks* en route *to Flint Castle.*

1. Start of the walk – Holywell town centre:
SJ 187760

Walk through the Tesco car park and follow a sloping concrete walkway into Greenfield Valley Heritage Park and pass under a large stone railway bridge.

2. Railway bridge:
SJ 187760

The footpath follows the line of a standard-gauge railway which, from 1912, carried passengers on the 'Little Train'. It was the steepest conventional passenger railway in Britain with a 1:27 gradient.

The path widens beyond the bridge and follows a stone wall down amongst deciduous woodland, now managed by the local wildlife trust. Along the way, you'll spot remnants of former industrial activity, with ruined buildings hidden amongst the trees to your left.

The woods are rich in wildlife with 27 different species of butterfly having been recorded. In amongst the trees, rare goshawks now nest and otters have been spotted living in the old mill workings and reservoirs.

At a bend in the trail, follow signs for St Winefride's Well and head past a bench and forested area with plenty of well-established, over-hanging trees.

Pass through a metal gate and walk down the hill, passing a furniture warehouse on your right. At the main road, turn left and follow the pavement along Greenfield Road towards St Winefride's Well.

3. St Winefride's Well:
SJ 185763

According to legend, the well first erupted at the spot where Winefride's would-be rapist, Caradog, cut off her head with his sword, back in the 7th century.

A spring rose from the ground where her head fell and her uncle, St Beuno, brought her back from the

Stained glass window at St Winefride's Well

dead through the power of prayer.

For centuries, pilgrims, including Richard I and Henry V, have visited the site to bathe in the holy water, known as the 'Lourdes of Wales'. Visitors can pay an entry fee and bathe in a swimming pool fed by the holy water, so take your bathers if you fancy a healing dip.

Walk back along the pavement to Greenfield valley, past the bench and turn left, following a yellow waymarker down the steep wooden steps to Greenfield Mills.

At the bottom of the steps, walk across the Royal Oak pub car park. Just before you reach the main road, turn right **(SJ 188766)** and follow a track down through the woods to the reservoir and ruined mill.

Greenfield Mill

4. Greenfield Mill: SJ 189767

Established in 1776, the Battery Works, as it was known, employed local people to literally bash out pots from brass sheets using heavy tilt hammers.

The works were powered by numerous water-wheels, so the noise here must have beendeafening during the manufacturing process.

Goods from the mill were exported from Liverpool to Africa and the money was used to buy slaves who worked the cotton fields in America. The cotton was then shipped back to Wales and to the cotton mills further down Greenfield valley.

The lake is now half as full as it was during the height of production, as the water upstream has since been diverted for other uses over the years.

During the winter months, pochard, tufted duck, little grebe, pintail and mandarin duck can be seen on the ponds.

Walk across the bridge towards a

tall chimney-stack at the edge of the woods and follow a path through the trees, past derelict buildings, in order to join the main path.

Turn left and walk down through the valley, passing another reservoir and Meadow Mill on your left.

5. Meadow Mill: SJ 191770

The mill, built in 1787, produced copper bolts and sheets used to sheath the wooden hulls of ships sailing to the tropics. The copper protected them against a timber-eating worm, hence the phrase 'copper-bottomed'.

The buildings left standing today were used for smaller industries, including a tinplate works.

Arriving at a crossroads, keep left, following an old wall. At the bottom, head past some black iron gates and keep right.

Walk towards Lower Cotton Mill, passing a pleasant lake before turning left at the bottom of the wooden steps. Cross over a footbridge for a closer look.

6. Lower Cotton Mill: SJ 193772

This is all that remains of the many cotton mills that once flourished here.

Abbey Wire Mill

The mill was originally a six-storey building, powered entirely by water-wheels fed, via culverts, by the Holywell stream.

The cotton mill closed in 1840 but reopened as a corn mill in 1850, producing flour until the early 1900s.

Retrace your route back up the steps and turn left onto the path. A little further on is the Abbey Wire Mill **(SJ 194773)** complete with a working water-wheel.

Today, the walled mill area is a pretty garden and venue for open-air events. Leave the garden and follow the quiet road opposite towards Greenfield Valley Museum – well worth a visit if you have time.

The museum consists of a number of historic buildings, all lovingly relocated and rebuilt on the site, so don't be confused if you see a

Victorian school-house next to a 16th century farmhouse.

Turn left behind the visitor centre (**SJ 195774**). At the end of the path, turn right and walk down to the abbey.

7. Basingwerk Abbey: SJ 196774

Basingwerk Abbey, which dates from 1132, is where Cistercian monks lived and worked for more than 400 years, harnessing the power of the stream to power their mills and grind corn. The impressive ruins are all that remain today.

During medieval times, the abbey flourished. An artistic community developed here which included many Welsh

Basingwerk Abbey

poets. The monks were finally driven out by Henry VIII's Dissolution Act of 1536.

Follow the path to the right, skirting the abbey and passing under some huge old sycamore trees down into the woods. Pass between two ornately carved wooden totem poles marking the entrance to the park and walk down into the car park below.

Turn left onto Bagillt Road (A548) then right at Dock Road. Walk up over the railway bridge

(SJ 198778). After a short stroll, turn left into Greenfields Docks.

8. Greenfield Docks: SJ 200779

There has been maritime activity here since Roman times but it wasn't until the legend of St Winefride's Well took hold that this quiet dock became busy as pilgrims flocked here from the Wirral, Liverpool and further afield.

As industry in the valley grew, the dock expanded and copper ore from Parys Mountain on Anglesey was unloaded here and sent to mills in the Greenfield valley to be turned into copper goods.

The arrival of the railway along the north coast and the continuing problems of silting up spelled the end of the dock, which was put up for sale in 1901.

In 2012 the dock was reopened and the Wales Coast Path, which is constantly being improved, now runs through it.

Walk past a large shipping buoy and head through a metal barrier onto the coast path.

From here you'll be rewarded with panoramic views across to Hilbre Island and the town of Hoylake on the opposite bank.

The factories that once thrived here have been demolished and much of the stone reused to create modern sea defences, the ultimate in recycling.

Along the estuary, the former waste ground is now home to a variety of wild flowers and shrubs, creating an ideal habitat for songbirds, migratory warblers, butterflies and short-eared owls, which can be seen hunting here in winter when the grass is shorter.

Art along the coastal path

During the winter months around 130,000 wading birds arrive at this internationally important site.

9. Viewing area: SJ 206774

Within the space of ½ mile you'll arrive at a curved viewing area overlooking a natural high-tide bird roost on the marsh below. The path had to be carefully re-routed here to avoid disturbing this vital habitat.

Proceed along the path and pass through a metal gate. Turn left and follow the signs for Bettisfield and Bagillt. This stretch is an excellent place to see oystercatchers feeding at low tide on the mudflats opposite.

Pass a community plaque set on a large stone and cross over an overflow pipe. Head through a metal kissing gate and continue along the embankment through two more gates **(SJ 206774)**.

Head down over a cattle access point, where cows come onto the salt marsh to feed, and through another gate **(SJ 211766)**.

Samphire in salt marshes

The route here is swathed in wild flowers, with hawthorn and elderberries in the autumn. Purple sea aster and samphire grow along the salt marsh during the summer.

If you notice an unusual red growth on the wild roses here, it's probably robin's pincushion, a pretty, red, fibrous growth containing the larvae of the gall wasp.

A little further on, walk past a turning and a patch of gorse, veer left down a sloping gravel track and through what was once a coal tip **(SJ 214762)**.

Walk straight along the track, past a railway bridge, through another gate and stop when you hear the sound of rushing water.

10. Milwr Tunnel: SJ 214761

The tunnel here is an outfall, built in the early 1900s, to drain the mine works on Halkyn Mountain near Holywell.

The tunnel stretched for 10 miles and drained more than 50 mineral veins, creating a labyrinth of more than 60 miles of interconnected passageways.

Water from the holy well also flows through here and local people refer to this spot as 'The Holy'.

Continue straight along a tarmac path, passing the old red brick pithead building on your right, which is now part of a scrap-metal business.

11. Bettisfield Colliery: SJ 215760

There were 11 coalmines in and around Bagillt during the 19th century with Bettisfield Colliery being the largest and most important, employing more than 500 men and producing both house and steam coal (used in steam trains and ships).

The pithead building would have housed the main winding engine house and winding shaft.

Amazingly, some mine shafts were dug under the estuary itself. Only two small pumps drained the water away, but no flooding was ever reported.

The best known mine, Point of Ayr Colliery further down the estuary, was one of the last deep coalmines in Wales and by 1953 was producing 213,000 tons of coal a year. It closed in 1996.

Turn left at the signpost for Bettisfield and walk towards a small inlet used by local fishermen.

12. Fisherman's inlet: SJ 216762

Local fishermen have fished here for generations, landing seasonal catches of cockles, shrimps and bass, an activity that has played a key role in the regeneration of the docks area.

Turn right and follow a grassy track towards an impressive dragon sculpture situated on top of a hill.

13. Dragon sculpture: SJ 217761

The sculpture is made from steel and has a beacon on its back which is lit, along with other beacons along the coast, during special events.

Walk down towards the pithead building **(SJ 216759)**. Pass through a kissing gate and along a landscaped path past a wooden sculpture of a miner known locally as Bettisfield Bob, which was stolen in 2011 and recovered from the top of Halkyn Mountain.

Veer left and follow the path running parallel to a minor road, a few yards from the railway line and the busy A548.

Fisherman's inlet

14. Halkyn marble gateposts: SJ 220756

A little further on, on your left hand side, you'll come across two gateposts made from local Halkyn Mountain marble. The fronts of the posts have been polished and sandblasted to create fish designs and when wet the real fossils beneath are revealed.

Walk along the track to the former Bagillt Docks and the inlet at Station Gutter.

15. Station Gutter: SJ 222754

The inlet, now silted up, used to be a very busy quay, exporting goods from the area around Bagillt, where lead smelting, coalmining, brewing and rope-making all took place.

At its peak, around 30 ships a day would dock here carrying lead, coal and copper, as well as passengers from Liverpool on their way to Denbigh and Flint.

Nowadays, the big ships sail past as they make their way from the Airbus wing factory at Broughton to Mostyn Dock and then on to Toulouse.

You may also see giant wind turbines being ferried down the estuary to windfarm sites.

Cross over a stone bridge and turn left towards Flint. Walk through a kissing gate and out along a track following a curving embankment with superb vistas over the golden sands, which glisten in the sun at low tide.

Opposite is the town of Parkgate where Lord Nelson and his mistress, Lady Hamilton, often stayed. She was from nearby Ness and used to bathe at Parkgate to cure a skin complaint.

Follow the trail along a long flat section known as Panton Cop for about ½ mile and down into a slight dip.

Keep left and walk up a slope, passing through a metal gate and up onto a narrow, enclosed pathway that brings you back alongside the sea. The track then widens as you pass through an area planted with native trees, shrubs and plenty of buddleia.

At a fork in the track, turn left (SJ 238741) and walk through a small wooded area of silver birch trees, emerging at Flint Point.

The Dee estuary

16. Flint Point: SJ 246740

Here you'll find another beacon which is lit for special events. There are magnificent views back up the estuary towards Greenfields and down river towards the Flintshire Bridge and Connah's Quay Power Station.

Keep right and follow the winding river around the inlet. At the end of the path turn left, and follow a short section of road down through a business park. Turn left again, back onto the coastal path and past the remains of Flint Dock.

17. Flint Dock: SJ 243736

The dock was built in the 1800s to export lead from Halkyn Mountain and later coal and timber as the boat yard developed. It's hard to believe but this quiet quayside was once not only the busiest place in Flint but also the dirtiest and most polluted due to the chemicals discharged here by heavy industry.

Follow a winding path around the dock and into the woods beyond, with glimpses of the estuary between the trees. Continue along the snaking route to Flint Castle.

18. Flint Castle: SJ 247734

This magnificent castle was the first of a series known as the 'iron ring', built during Edward I's campaign to conquer Wales.

It was built in a strategic position, only one day's march from Chester and easily resupplied by boat.

It's had a colourful past, having been attacked by Welsh forces under the command of Dafydd ap Gruffydd, brother of Llywelyn ap Gruffydd, the last native prince of Wales, and attacked again in 1294 during the revolt of Madog ap Llywelyn.

During the English Civil War, Flint Castle was held by the Royalists before being captured by the Parliamentarians in 1647 after a three month siege.

Oliver Cromwell later ordered the castle to be destroyed to prevent its reuse although the ruins that remain are substantial.

The castle marks the end of this walk along the magnificent Dee estuary. Flint town centre is just around the corner, where there is a regular bus service taking you back to the starting point in Holywell.

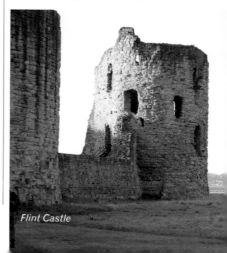

Flint Castle

Derek says. . .

THIS WALK IN LAUGHARNE is a real gem and follows in the footsteps of the great poet and playwright, Dylan Thomas. According to Dylan, 'there's nowhere like it anywhere at all' and I can see why. Laugharne is an enchanting village with an impressive 12th century castle overlooking Carmarthen Bay.

The walk takes you on a poetic journey, passing the places and landscapes that inspired Dylan's poetry, and the cemetery of St Martin's Church where he is buried along with his wife Caitlin.

The Boathouse, where he did most of his writing, is now a popular museum. You can have a cuppa and a Welsh cake here, learn more about his life and enjoy the stunning view of the Taf estuary.

The walk also leads you onto the path known as 'Dylan's Birthday Walk' created by local farmer Bob Stevens. From Sir John's Hill you are treated to gorgeous views of Gower, Tenby, Caldey Island and north Devon.

Back in town, take a look around the Tin Shed Experience, which is a quaint and quirky 1940s museum.

The year 2014 marks the 100th anniversary of Dylan's birth and celebrations are planned in Laugharne. Another date for your diary is the arts and literary festival, which takes place every April.

12. Laugharne

Approximate distance: 4½ miles

Laugharne

Distance: 4½ miles

Map: *OS Explorer Map 177*

Introduction: *A 4½ mile circular walk around the small, historic town of Laugharne, situated on the estuary of the River Taf in Carmarthenshire. The walk is fairly easy and comprises of two short loops forming a figure-of-eight with the town at its centre.*

Along the way, you'll pass the town hall where the Corporation and its Portreeve have been in control since medieval times. From there, the route heads past Brown's Hotel and along the estuary, passing Dylan Thomas's boathouse and Laugharne Castle before following 'Dylan's Birthday Walk' through the woods and over St John's Hill back to the town.

1. Start of the walk: Grist car park: SH 681066

The walk begins in the Grist car park in the shadow of Laugharne Castle. The Grist is an open area of reclaimed land, where the River Corran meets the sea and its name probably derives from a former corn or grist mill that once stood at the mouth of the river.

From the car park, head towards the main road and turn right, walking up a slight incline towards the castle entrance, passing the pink castle house as you head towards the clock tower, approximately 200 yards up the road.

Public toilets are located halfway up the road, on the right hand side, – you'll need a 20p coin if you want to use them.

2. Town Hall and Clock Tower: SN 302108

This lovely old whitewashed building, complete with clock tower, has been the headquarters of Laugharne Corporation for centuries. The Corporation, which pre-dates Parliament, is a unique medieval institution established in 1297 by Sir Guy de Brian, a Marcher Lord.

The Corporation is presided over by the Portreeve, who generally serves for a couple of years before new elections are held. Each Portreeve

gets to wear a traditional gold chain of cockleshells, with their name and date of service inscribed on the back.

Today the Corporation deals with civil cases and land disputes and has many ancient customs, including the Beating of the Bounds. This particular tradition takes place every three years and is a 25-mile romp across the Corporation's land.

At significant landmarks along the way, a person is selected and asked to name the exact location. If they cannot answer correctly, they are hoisted upside down and spanked three times on the bottom! Perhaps it's not surprising that Dylan was inspired here to create his eccentric cast of characters in *Under Milk Wood*.

3. Brown's Hotel: SN 302109

Continue up through the town, stopping at one of Dylan Thomas's favourite watering holes, Brown's Hotel, which is now a stylish boutique hotel, thanks to restoration grants.

Dylan Thomas could often be seen sat by the window, writing, drinking and chatting to the landlady, whilst observing the town's characters as they went about their daily business.

Dylan's parents lived opposite in Pelican House, with its formidable black front door and big brass knocker. It was here that Dylan's body was laid out prior to his funeral in 1953.

As you wander along the main street you'll begin to notice the varied styles of architecture and grandiose Georgian houses, uncharacteristic of other Welsh towns in the area.

This was due to the fact that the Georgians began to visit Laugharne and treat it as a kind of spa resort once the railway line had reached Carmarthen. As a result, the town prospered.

Laugharne is back on the map as a tourist destination today – largely thanks to Dylan.

Take care when walking along the narrow pavements and particularly when crossing the roads. Despite its size, Laugharne is a busy little place with plenty of holiday traffic and large delivery lorries navigating the narrow road in and out of town.

4. Tin Shed Museum: SN 302112

Heading into Clifton Street, you'll arrive at the 1940s Tin Shed Museum which specialises in 1940s cameras and WWII memorabilia. They've supplied a number of TV productions and Hollywood epics, including *Saving Private Ryan* and *Band of Brothers*, with vintage camera equipment.

5. St Martin's Church and Dylan Thomas's grave: SN 302114

Leaving the Tin Shed Museum, walk a short distance along the road to St Martin's Church, where Dylan Thomas and his wife Caitlin are buried.

Walk through the lych-gate and up the track towards the church building. Turn right and cross a footbridge leading into the cemetery.

Dylan's grave is a very simple white, wooden cross located in the middle of the cemetery, towards the top of the field.

At the back of the cemetery is an old iron kissing gate. Head through, turn left and then right and onto a quiet country lane **(SN 302115)**.

6. Ant's Lane: SN 302120

Head on for about ½ mile until you reach a farm, signposted Delacourse Uchaf farmhouse.

Follow the road around the bend and turn right into Ant's Lane, leading to Delacourse Isaf. The lane is signposted and, along the way, you'll pass a wooden sign labelled 'Delacorse'.

Heading down a rough overgrown track, you'll quickly find yourself in the midst of a pretty wood with overhanging trees – a million miles away from the hustle and bustle of Laugharne!

7. Delacourse Isaf: SN 307122

Within ½ mile or so you'll come to a clearing next to Delacourse Isaf, an impressive house with outbuildings and well-stocked garden.

The track, part of the Wales Coastal Path, is signposted and you'll soon catch your first glimpse of the coast in the shape of the tranquil Taf estuary.

Walk down the lane past the house and gardens, passing through a metal gate and into open countryside. Ahead, you'll cross over a wooden stile next to a lovely old tree.

Keep left, skirting the bottom of a steep hill, a pleasant spot to stop for a break.

Nowadays, thousands of pilgrims arrive in the town to pay homage to Dylan Thomas but in centuries past, religious pilgrims passed through here on their way to St Davids. Just down river from here were two popular ferry crossing points.

After a brief section of open ground, you'll head into woods along a track above the estuary, passing en route derelict stone houses, relics of the cockle industry that once flourished here.

The track is wide and has been well-used for centuries but does have steep drops, so be careful where you're treading.

After ten minutes or so you'll be back in civilisation, passing below Laugharne Park caravan fields and following a tarmac path leading towards the Dylan Thomas Boathouse.

8. Dylan Thomas Boathouse: SN 306110

Dylan and his wife Caitlin lived in the Boathouse, overlooking the Taf estuary, with their children, Aeronwy, Llewelyn and Colm, from 1949 to 1953.

The Boathouse, owned by Carmarthenshire County Council, is now a museum with authentic furnishings and memorabilia. Looking out over the estuary, you

This part of the estuary was once a busy harbour, exporting goods all around the globe. Nowadays the Taf estuary is part of the Carmarthen Bay Special Area of Conservation and is a Site of Special Scientific Interest.

9. Laugharne Castle: SN 302107

begin to understand why Dylan fell in love with the area, with its magnificent views.

Nearby is the quaint little writing shed where Dylan spent much of his time.

Follow the path known as Dylan's Walk back towards the town, turning right into Cliff Road. Turn left into Victoria Street and walk down Market Lane, passing the Seaview Hotel on your right **(SN 303108)**. Dylan and Caitlin once lived in this house too.

At the end of Market Lane, turn left at Tŷ'r Goets and then right, following the path down to the castle and estuary.

The castle was first established in 1116 by the invading Normans and then attacked and retaken countless times by the Welsh. It was later enlarged and the towering walls you see today are additions to the original building.

Oliver Cromwell laid siege to the castle during the Civil War and the dents made in the walls by the Roundheads can still be seen today.

Beyond the castle, cross over the stream and head through the car park, where you began the walk, towards Dylan's Birthday Walk, passing a wooden sculpture of Dylan Thomas en route.

Laugharne Castle

10. Dylan's Birthday Walk: SN 302104

Follow The Strand beside the salt marsh and go up into the woods, taking in the views and reading the information boards as you go. There are a few steep sections here and the ground is uneven, so take your time.

This marked trail through 'Milk Wood' was inspired by 'A Poem in October', a poem Dylan Thomas wrote on his 30th birthday. As you walk along the path in Dylan's footsteps, the poem describes the view before you.

Local farmer Bob Stevens created this walk with the hope of making Laugharne the world's first 'birthday town', where visitors walk the trail on their birthday every year and read Thomas's words, handily written out on the information boards: 'O may my heart's truth still be sung on this high hill in a year's turning'.

Whether you're into poetry or not, don't miss out on this section of the walk, as the views a little further on are stunning as you look over towards the castle with the estuary and salt marsh below you.

Along the route you'll find view points and benches to sit and enjoy the scenery.

The salt marshes, edged by golden sands at low tide, are characterised by intricate patterns carved out of them by the ebb and flow of the tide.

The mudflats are rich in wildlife with various kinds of visiting wading birds and the occasional peregrine falcon might fly by.

It's a fascinating landscape. Some of this land has been reclaimed from the sea by means of a series of drainage ditches or 'reens' built in the 1600s.

You can clearly spot two distinct shades of grass: one, salt-encrusted and washed out and covered daily by the high tide; the other, a luscious green colour, protected by a sea wall from the salt water and home to grazing cattle.

11. The Last Verse

Within 10 minutes or so, you'll arrive at a lovely wooden signpost carved with the words 'The Last Verse' and a bench bearing the words 'summery on the hill's shoulder'.

Follow the path left, down the hill to the last information panel. If it happens to be your birthday say out loud 'The Last Verse' and sit and contemplate a year's turning, enjoying the panoramic views towards Ginst Point, Gower and north Devon.

Retrace your footsteps back up the hill to the wooden 'Last Verse' sign and turn left.

The path along here can get a bit muddy but there are no real hazards.

Down in the dip to your left, you might catch a glimpse of the sea wall and the odd boat or two that Bob has salvaged.

After a while, you'll spot a way-marker, 'To Laugharne over Sir John's Hill', which guides you off to the right. Follow the wooden steps up the hillside towards the stile and make your way into the fields above.

Take care along this stretch as the wooden steps and track can be a bit slippery under foot.

12. Sir John's Hill: SN 302098

You'll now be standing at the bottom left hand side of a large field.

Head north towards a hedge at the top left hand side of the field and climb over a stone stile if the gate is closed **(SN 301099)**.

If you veer off to the left, following the hedge line along to a farm gate **(SN 230099)** you'll be able to see a medieval field system (notice the green strips of land) in the fields over to the right, leading up the hill.

Alternatively, just follow the track diagonally through the field to the far right hand side where you'll pick up the path again.

13. End of the walk – return to the Grist: SN 301100

Climb over a wooden stile and turn left at the road. The last section is roughly ½ mile long, following a quiet wooded lane.

Just before you reach the A4066, turn right down Back Lane. Follow the lane back to the estuary and Grist car park where the walk began.

View from Sir John's Hill

Derek says. . .

MANY PEOPLE who visit Llanberis come to climb Snowdon but if you fancy a change from the iconic mountain or something less demanding and less busy, then this walk would be a good choice.

This 4 mile circular walk has a few steep ups and downs but the scenery is breathtaking with towering mountains, massive slate tips and cracking views over Llyn Padarn and Llanberis.

There's no shortage of history either, including an ancient oak forest and the remains of Dolbadarn Castle which dates back to the 13th century.

The walk follows in the footsteps of quarrymen who lived and worked on the mountainside. If you can, take a peek around the old quarry hospital which is like walking into a time capsule.

If you look very closely, you can see the face of a lady on one of the hillsides. It took me a while but eventually I did see it. On a clear day, the summit of Snowdon is also visible on this delightful walk.

The Dinorwig hydroelectric power station is close by too – the largest scheme of its kind in Europe. The visitor centre runs tours which allow you to see the massive pump and turbines in action.

13. Llanberis slate walk

Llanberis slate walk

Approximate distance: 4 miles

Great Welsh Walks

Distance: 4 miles

Map: *OS Explorer Map: OL17*

Introduction: *This 4 mile circular walk takes you through the very heart of the Padarn Country Park and Dinorwig slate quarries. The backdrop of Snowdon and Llyn Padarn make this a truly spectacular walk. The walk begins on flat ground, taking in Dolbadarn Castle, the National Slate Museum, Llanberis Lake Railway and the old quarry hospital. However, it soon becomes more challenging as you follow a rough and winding track up through ancient sessile oak woodland towards giant slate tips and quarries. It's then a steep descent down the final incline until you reach the road taking you back to the start.*

1. Start of the walk – Llanberis Lake Railway station: SH 582599

The walk begins outside the Llanberis Lake Railway station and not at the nearby popular Snowdon Mountain Railway.

There is plenty of parking near the Snowdon Mountain Railway and opposite the path leading to Dolbadarn Castle.

Follow the signs for Dolbadarn Castle and the National Slate Museum and, opposite a car park, turn right. Cross a large slate footbridge over the River Hwch and follow a winding track up through the woods to the castle.

2. Dolbadarn Castle: SH 586598

The castle overlooking Llyn Peris was built by the Welsh prince, Llywelyn the Great during the early 13th century to control the Llanberis Pass – it's a strategic location, protecting trade and military routes into north and mid Wales. Entry to the castle is free and it's worth exploring.

The castle's round keep is said to mimic the Norman castle at Pembroke.

Edward I and his army took the castle in 1284 and it gradually fell into disrepair. The ruins were popular with 18th and 19th century artists and were famously painted by Turner in 1802.

Retrace your steps as far as the road. Turn right and head towards the

Dolbadarn Castle

National Slate Museum and the 'Electric Mountain' hydro power station.

Crossing between the lakes, you'll get your first glimpse of the views to come, with the mountains and Llanberis Pass looming in the distance.

Turn left at the mini-roundabout and walk towards the National Slate Museum.

3. The National Slate Museum: SH 586602

Dinorwig Quarry closed in 1969 but the Victorian workshops, with the largest working waterwheel in Britain were preserved.

The Industrial Revolution of the 19th century led to an explosion of towns and cities across the country and saw demand take off for slate as a roofing material. It was also exported across the developing world.

In 1882 Caernarfonshire's quarries produced more than 280,000 tons of finished roofing slates and in 1898 the slate trade in Wales reached its peak with 17,000 men producing 485,000 tons of slate. Entry to the museum is free.

Vivian Quarry

4. Vivian Quarry: SH 587605

From the museum, walk across the railway track and through the railway barrier-gate towards the old Vivian Quarry, last worked in 1958.

Pass through a large stone archway, emerging inside the quarry, littered with old industrial buildings.

When production stopped, the lower half of the quarry gradually flooded to form a deep, blue lake – up to 18m deep in places and now popular with scuba divers.

Follow a winding track along to the lakeside viewing platform for a closer look.

These days, rock climbers also come here to scale the slate slabs, and you can see some of the climbing routes dotted around the sheer rock faces.

Retrace your steps back to the front of the museum and walk over to the far side of the car park, passing a café, toilets and gift shop **(SH 585605)**.

Follow a path of slate chippings towards the lake and along a winding track up to a grassy viewpoint below the old quarry hospital (**SH 583606**).

There are nice views here over the lake and you'll regularly hear and see the steam train carrying passengers on a scenic trip along the lake shore.

Walk up the wooden steps towards the former hospital and marvel at the fascinating old photographs and medical equipment inside.

Quarry Hospital

5. Quarry Hospital: SH 583607

The hospital here was for the men who worked at the Dinorwig Quarry in the 19th and 20th centuries. The idea was to have a hospital on site so that the injured could get back to work as soon as possible after treatment.

The hospital treated a range of injuries, from broken bones to crush injuries, and employed the latest medical techniques of the time.

They were even equipped with an X-ray machine, just three years after its invention in Germany. It was also one of the first buildings in the area to have both hot and cold running water and electricity.

Turn left out of the hospital and follow a tarmac road through the entrance gates. Turn left up a rough track of slate chippings, signposted as the green route, and head up a winding track into the ancient woodlands above.

6. Sessile oak woodlands: SH 584607

The woods here date back to the time of Dolbadarn Castle and were once known as the Royal Forest of Gwynedd, stocked with deer and wild boar for royal hunting.

These days you'll find wild goats roaming the sessile oak woodland, the trees of which are stunted due to the lack of nutrients in the soil. Sessile oaks are characterised by stalkless acorns that grow from their branches.

The track is covered in slate and tree roots so take care, especially in the wet. As you ascend, the oaks become noticeably smaller in height. About halfway up, you'll reach a viewpoint overlooking the lake below. From here continue up the track, following the green/yellow route.

As you approach a green/yellow sign with a red marker post, keep right and follow the yellow route up the hill, over a slate step and through a gap in an old wall, as you head towards a triangular shaped clearing in the trees with a green post in the middle.

Keep right and follow the yellow/blue route up a muddy track leading to Coed Dinorwig. Walk past an information board onto a gravel path and into a clearing, leaving the woods behind you.

Opposite you now are rolling green hills and cottages where quarrymen once lived and rented small plots of land on which to grow vegetables and keep livestock.

Walk along a rough 4x4 track passing a house and stables as you head towards some large slate tips in the distance (**SH 584611**).

The slate tips are an incredible sight and are the end product of a very wasteful industry. A staggering 80–90% of slate mined here was waste.

'Electric Mountain' power station

About 600m ahead, cross the road and walk past a commemorative slate statue to the former quarry workers, before passing through a metal gate. Walk along a winding track marked 'slate trails', past a wonderful old slate wall draped in thick green moss and on towards the quarries.

The track soon widens and, if it's sunny, you'll be rewarded with a stunning vista of the mountains beyond.

7. View Point: SH 591604

On a clear day, you can see the summit of Snowdon from here and, looking carefully, you'll just make out the Snowdon Mountain Railway track as it winds its way up the mountain from Llanberis.

To your left are the old quarry workings and mills where the slate was initially cut and dressed into roofing slates.

Turn right and follow the path down to a viewing area and take a few moments to enjoy the scenery around you.

Below and to your left is the entrance to the Dinorwig Power Station, built deep inside Elidir Fawr **(SH 591604)**.

The station's six powerful generating units stand in Europe's largest man-made cavern, 23m wide, 180m long and 51m tall, which you can visit on an organised tour.

The power station known as 'Electric Mountain' is used to top up the National Grid during times of peak demand, famously during

Views towards Snowdon

half-time in an FA Cup Final when millions of kettles are switched on simultaneously.

Turn right through a rusty kissing gate and follow a tramway incline down the mountain. Wagons loaded with slate were lowered down the incline from the quarry to the finishing mill below.

8. The Incline: SH 592605

There were three main inclines, with the highest being over 1500ft above sea level and home to the highest locomotive shed in Britain.

Take care walking down the first section as the slate can be slippery, even on dry days. It's a fairly surreal experience walking between thousands of tonnes of discarded slate, seemingly balanced precariously on either side of the incline.

You can still spot traces of the original tram tracks here and there along the incline, and ahead you'll pass under a drum house, once used to control the speed of the wagons as they were lowered down the mountainside.

The Incline

One rope was attached to a rake of loaded wagons at the top and the other rope fastened to empty wagons below. By skilful use of the brake on the drum, the loaded wagons going down hauled the empty wagons up.

Follow the incline down until you reach the former quarrymen's cottages on the right hand side of the track.

9. Anglesey Barracks: SH 590602

The two rows of terraced cottages, eleven on each side, were known as the Anglesey Barracks as they housed workers from Anglesey who stayed here during the working week.

Life was hard and very basic with four men crammed into each small cottage. Despite having no running water and only a coal fire for heating and cooking, the barracks were a hive of cultural activities, including choir singing and poetry reading.

The men would leave for home at noon each Saturday and arrive back early on Monday morning ready to start work.

The cottages were condemned as a health hazard in 1948, by which time most workers were already living in better conditions and using buses each day to travel to work from further afield.

Continue down the incline – with views of Llyn Peris and the power station below – taking care as you walk between the tracks overgrown with grass.

Follow a high slate wall as it curves its way around a wooded area towards another drum house. Here you'll find huge pieces of slate overhanging the wall, which served as a makeshift shelter for the workers during bad weather.

Llyn Padarn

On a sunny day it's very pleasant here but in winter, during heavy rain or blizzards, it must have been incredibly cold and bleak.

10. Former brake house: SH 588602

Within the remains of the brake house on the left, you'll find a curiously shaped window, aligned diagonally through the wall in such a way as to give the brakeman inside an excellent view of the approaching slate wagons.

Keep right and follow the slate steps for a few yards before turning left at the gap in the wall. Cross over an old iron footbridge, above the brake house.

From the bridge you'll have magnificent views west over the town, and up the valley towards the Llanberis Pass.

There are fantastic photo opportunities from up here, especially looking down over Dolbadarn Castle.

Follow a zigzagging path, bordered by an impressive slate wall, drop down between the slate tips and along a clearly marked track through a short section of oak woodland.

Take care, as the ground is uneven with loose stones. You'll also need to negotiate the odd steep section but there are wooden steps provided along the trickier parts.

Emerging at the bottom, you'll find yourself on a tarmac road. Keep right and follow the road back towards the National Slate Museum.

Just beyond the railway track, turn left and walk over a footbridge spanning the River Rhythallt **(SH 586602)**.

End of the walk – back to Llanberis Lake Railway station: SH 582599

Follow a level path running parallel to the railway track for about ½ mile that takes you back to the Llanberis Lake Railway station and the end of the walk.

Derek says. . .

THERE IS SOMETHING for everyone on this fabulous walk in the Millennium Coastal Park which attracts more than one million visitors each year. The coastline, once dominated by heavy industry, has been completely transformed and now boasts woodlands, marinas, cycle paths and walkways.

This 11 mile walk is a journey through time passing the sites of the lost villages of Machynys and Bwlch y Gwynt. The land once occupied by terraced houses and a tinplate works is now an 18-hole championship golf course.

This walk is easily accessible because it's only 15 minutes from the M4 motorway. It's also nice and flat and quite wide too, making it suitable for wheelchair users.

The Loughor estuary is one of the most important areas in Wales for wildfowl and wading birds, so bring your binoculars.

If time allows, drop into the National Wetlands Centre, which is well worth a visit. And don't forget your camera – on a clear day the views across the water to north Gower are glorious.

One of the most famous visitors to Burry Port was pilot Amelia Earhart who landed there on June 17th 1928, having completed her first transatlantic flight. Check out the monument overlooking the harbour, which commemorates the event.

14. Loughor Estuary

Approximate distance: 11 miles

Loughor Estuary

Start

eserved. Ordnance Survey Licence number 100019855

Great Welsh Walks

Distance: 11 miles

Map: *OS Explorer Map 164*

Introduction: *A long, flat, 11 mile trek along the Loughour estuary via the Millennium Coastal Park from Bynea Gateway to the old harbour at Pembrey. Along the way, you'll pass beside the National Wetlands Centre, an important area for wading birds over winter. Heading along the coast, you'll also pass the relics of a lost community from a bygone age and a legendary monastic retreat before arriving at the former docks in Llanelli. It's then on to Sandy Water Park, a former industrial area now transformed into parkland and lakes, before you dock at the revamped Burry Port harbour and finish at the old harbour at Pembrey, next to Wales's longest beach, Cefn Sidan.*

1. Start of the walk – Millennium Coastal Park: SS 554984

To get here by car, take Junction 47 off the M4 and head west along the A484 towards Llanelli. Drive over the Loughor Bridge and take the second exit on the roundabout, following signs for the Bynea Gateway car park.

The walk starts by following the coast path west around the corner for about 200m and over a large metal footbridge spanning the A484 and railway track **(SS 553984)**.

From the bridge you'll be rewarded with your first views of the Burry Inlet and northern stretch of the Loughor estuary with its pristine salt marsh habitat and large tidal range.

2. Views over the Loughor estuary: SS 552982

The estuary is a Special Area of Protection and is noted for its large variety of wildlife, particularly birds.

Each winter, waders and wildfowl flock here to feed on the nutrient-rich mudflats. The estuary contains the most extensive salt marsh in Wales (2,200 hectares).

At low tide extensive areas of the estuary are exposed and support a thriving cockle industry.

Away from busy main road, the estuary, on a calm day, is a serene place blessed with glassy reflections and picture-postcard views.

Cross over three wooden footbridges

and walk past the Gateway Holiday Park towards the National Wetlands Centre.

The path turns to the right after ½ mile, taking you behind the old sea wall and onto a lane bordering the wetlands reserve.

Follow the road for about 1 mile, past a derelict building on your left, opposite which are large piles of rock **(SS 533982)**.

It's then a short stroll down a quiet wooded lane to the entrance to the National Wetlands Centre.

3. National Wetlands Centre: SS 531984

Set in a 450 acre mosaic of lakes, pools and lagoons, the reserve is home to many thousands of wild and native species, as well as imported ones such as the rather bizarre Caribbean flamingo.

The man-made reserve is managed by the Wildfowl and Wetlands Trust. It opened its doors to the public in 1991 and was extended as part of the Millennium Coastal Path project.

During the winter months roughly 50,000 birds visit the Burry Inlet, stopping off to feed at the reserve's lagoons and shallow pools.

During the summer, you can hear sedge, reed and Cetti's warblers along this stretch of the walk.

Pass the entrance and cross over the road **(SS 533986)** following signs for the Park Centre (4 miles) and walk through a wooden gateway onto a wide gravel track.

Ahead you'll soon spot the Trostre steel works beyond the railway line opposite **(SS 526988)**.

Turn left onto a long straight section of track that runs alongside the Machynys golf course.

Walk further on and you'll find

a wooden art installation and observation platform with views over the sea wall towards the estuary.

You'll lose sight of the estuary as you head through a sheltered section below the sea wall along the edge of the golf course.

This is a good spot for wildlife, so keep an eye out for otters, water voles, kingfishers and butterflies along the edge of the stream.

Some way ahead the track splits into two near a picnic area **(SS 519980)**. Take the left hand track leading down to the estuary and cross over a footbridge and a white gate which acts as a tidal flap to control the water levels.

The route now hugs the edge of the green salt marsh.

The estuary itself is a Site of Special Scientific Interest (SSSI) within the Carmarthen Bay Special Area of Conservation.

Look out for small flocks of dunlin, ringed plover, sanderling and redshank along the coast. Shelduck, oystercatcher and curlew can be seen further out on the mudflats.

Ahead you'll soon notice some old buildings – known locally as 'the butts' – that were constructed for target practice during the Second World War.

Follow the path past a lake with sweeping views over the estuary, towards north Gower and the Whiteford lighthouse – an unusual cast-iron lighthouse that stands in splendid isolation in the channel.

4. Machynys (Monk's Island): SS 512976

Local legend has it that in 513 AD the holy man, St Piro, built a monastery on an island in the Loughor estuary, known as Mynach Ynys. It is thought to have been located in this general area but vanished over time.

There is little evidence of its physical existence, but it's known that a grand house stood on Machynys for a considerable time. Apparently, it even had a tunnel running from a cellar and on underneath the estuary, which was used to cross over to north Gower.

When the steel, copper and tinplate industries were established in the area, more land was needed, so a sea wall was built and the tidal marsh was drained and filled in, turning the former island into a peninsula.

The land now forms part of the Machynys championship golf course.

There are various little tracks leading down onto the banks of estuary here but, take care if the tide is pushing in, as the waters here are extremely treacherous with strong currents as the tide ebbs and flows.

Follow the path around a wide sandy lagoon scattered with sea-grass until you arrive at a modern housing development, where the village of Bwlch y Gwynt stood for nearly 100 years.

5. Bwlch y Gwynt: SS 509978

The industrialisation of the Machynys area began around 1841 with the construction of the South Wales Iron and Tin Works.

This entire coast was once engulfed by heavy industry, with steelworks, chemical factories, brickworks, tinplate works and large docks.

The peninsula here had its own community, known as Bwlch y Gwynt, which consisted of several rows of terraced cottages where factory and mill workers lived.

The homes were demolished in the 1970s and the residents rehoused in nearby Morfa and other parts of south Llanelli.

Nowadays, the only buildings here are modern housing estates, such as Pentre Nicklaus, with expansive sea views. A blue plaque and information board commemorates the former community of Bwlch y Gwynt.

Continue along the coast past a modern lighthouse sculpture and blue plaque commemorating Machynys Farm.

Walk past a modern housing estate and walk around another small bay to join up with a cycle route. Some way ahead, turn right and follow signs for Cycle Route 4 **(SS 503985)**.

A track takes you back to civilisation and along the busy B4304 road to Llanelli, crossing over a blue footbridge and a roundabout signposted Copperhouse.

Follow the path parallel to the road that leads to the old North Dock.

6. North Dock: SS 499995

Large ships once docked here, importing and exporting goods associated with the flourishing steel and tinplate industry, which led to the town being known as Tre'r Sosban, the town of saucepans.

A sea wall was built in the estuary here to direct the flow of the river towards the dock in order to prevent it from silting up, but the dock was eventually abandoned in the 1950s.

Turn left and cross the road bridge, past the dock opposite, which is now used for recreation and water-sports, with housing along its edges.

Up ahead is the Discovery Centre, a contemporary building designed to resemble a large white ship.

7. The Discovery Centre: SS 497994

This building has panoramic views over the estuary and Gower and is an ideal stopping-off point with a café, toilets, tourist information and bike hire available.

From the centre, the walk continues along the estuary, following a winding cycle track through green landscaped hillocks complete with angling lakes and art installations.

Ahead of the visitor centre stands a mound overlooking Sandy Water Park with a commemorative plaque on the top.

8. Sandy Water Park: SN 494003

This section of the park played a crucial part in the rebirth of the Llanelli coastline and was the first of the main regeneration projects, showing how a former industrial area can be reinvigorated.

The 16 acre lake is now a wildlife haven and lies adjacent to the Festival Fields **(SN 491005)** where the National Eisteddfod was held in 2000.

A circle of Gorsedd stones marks the spot where several of the Eisteddfod ceremonies took place **(SS 497994)**.

Head along the coast past the fishing lakes, one of which is a championship lake that attracts anglers from all over the world **(SN 479008)**.

The reed beds are home to mute swans, mallards, tufted ducks, grebes and moorhens and are a stronghold for the rare yellow brimstone butterfly.

Eventually, after passing a cricket pitch, continue straight on, ignoring a right turn which leads you up past another small lake.

Further ahead, follow the path around a right hand bend and take the path to the left. Walk down to a railway bridge and cross over.

Gorsedd stones

Continue along a winding track past a small fishing lake, opposite which is a sculpted mound of earth that appears to curl its way towards you in the form of a peninsula.

9. The earth sculpture: SN 461004

The earth sculpture called 'Walking with the Sea' is known locally as Teletubbies Mountain and was designed to be visible from land, sea and air. Two new beaches have formed on its western and eastern edges.

Continue past three more lakes and a rollerblade park **(SN 451002)** towards Burry Port Harbour.

Along the way, you can see the route of the old coastal path which was washed away by a combination of high spring tides and a violent storm in March 2008.

The new path takes you slightly inland, away from the sea, but not for long as you'll soon arrive back at the coast, alongside the car park and slipway. Turn right and walk along the sea front to the harbour.

10. Burry Port Harbour: SN 446003

Burry Port was born out of the industrial revolution and the need to export coal from nearby valleys to the rest of the world.

More than £8 million has been spent on converting the tidal harbour into a modern marina with water levels being controlled by an automatic tidal gate.

Although silting continues to be a problem, one apparent benefit is a new beach now covering former mudflats, making Cefn Padrig a popular destination for day-trippers.

In 1928 Amelia Earhart landed here in her seaplane *Friendship*, becoming the first woman to fly across the Atlantic. Her plane was towed into the harbour where you can still find reminders of this pioneering flight, including the original wooden buoy it was moored to.

At the marina, turn right, walk down past the lifeboat building and then turn left.

Views across the estuary to north Gower

Pembrey Old Harbour

Make your way around the harbour and walk across two footbridges.

On a paved area between the bridges is an inscription commemorating Amelia Earhart's historic visit.

The old west dock, to the right, has an unusually rich diversity of wild flowers growing along the old walls, including the rare small-flowered catchfly, rock samphire, sea lavender and round-leaved crane's bill.

There's usually a mobile food van in the car park here, should you require some sustenance.

To get a closer look at the picturesque lighthouse, take a detour by turning left and walking down the other side of the harbour **(SN 444000)**.)

Walk straight on in a westerly direction past a few houses at Chandler's Yard and turn left, following signs for the coast path towards a sandy track.

Where the path splits, turn right and follow the path down between sand-dunes and the Shoreline Leisure Park.

Along the way you may wish to follow a boardwalk down onto the beach, or just keep going as we did.

Continue walking as far as a tidal lagoon and then take the path leading to the old harbour wall. It's then a short stroll to the end of the harbour for some amazing views.

11. End of the walk – Pembrey Old Harbour: SS 437999

The old harbour is perched right on the edge of the estuary with panoramic views across to Gower, Carmarthen Bay and the southern tip of Cefn Sidan.

Cefn Sidan, which forms part of Pembrey Country Park, is an 8 mile long, award winning beach. In fact, it is Wales's longest beach, renowned for its fine sand and a favourite of sun worshippers, swimmers and walkers.

The harbour was built in 1819, during the coalmining boom, but suffered from silting and was replaced by Pembrey New Dock (now called Burry Port Harbour) a few decades later.

Our walk ends here. You can catch a train from Pembrey and Burry Port station (just off the B4311) back to Brynea station (just over ½ mile north of the start point/car park), or hop on a local bus which stops along the B4297 near the start point.

Derek says. . .

I LOVE NORTH WALES with its coast, valleys, mountains and moors and this 6 mile trek in the county of Conwy allows you to experience them all.

The climb up from Penmaenmawr may leave you out of breath, but you are soon rewarded with spectacular views along the coast towards Anglesey, Puffin Island, and the Great Orme.

Quarrymen used to take this route on their way to work, including Huw Tom who later became known as the unofficial prime minister of Wales. You pass the house where he lived as a boy, from which there are fine views of the Conwy valley and the Clwydian hills in the distance.

There are several points of interest on this walk, including an Iron Age hillfort and Maen y Bardd (stone of the bard), a cromlech or burial chamber more than 3,000 years old. Legend has it that a giant threw his spear across the valley at his dog which was sheltering in the chamber.

On reaching the pretty village of Rowen, there is a friendly pub, the Tŷ Gwyn, where we stopped for lunch. If you time your walk well, you can hop on a bus back to the start of the walk in Penmaenmawr.

15. Penmaenmawr

Approximate distance: 6 miles

Distance: 6 miles
Map: *OS Explorer Map OL17*
Introduction: *A strenuous 6 mile linear walk from Penmaenmawr up into the hills following the Huw Tom Upland Walk before dropping down into the idyllic village of Rowen. Along the way you'll see ancient standing stones and cairns, stunning views over the River Conwy, old settlements and an Iron Age hillfort.*
Penmaenmawr lies between Conwy and Bangor and is partly within the Snowdonia National Park. It is renowned for its spectacular mountain and coastal walks as well as the nearby Bwlch Sychnant (Sychnant Pass) and Mynydd y Dref.
Before the 1830s the town was small, with a population of about 200 people, but within 20 years this had increased to more than 4,000 thanks to the area's Victorian seaside resort status, the railway and the quarrying industry.

1. Start of the walk – New York Cottages: SH 718766

The walk begins a few hundred yards west of the town centre where you'll find some terraced houses, known as the New York Cottages, on the main Bangor road. These terraced houses were built in the 1840s to house workers from the nearby Graiglwyd Quarry.

At the time, many of the workers were leaving Wales for New York in search of work, hence the name, and house number 4 is now a small museum documenting the local quarrying industry.

If you stand on the bridge opposite and peer over the edge, you can still see the old quarry conveyor line, used to transport quarried stone off the mountain and down to the jetty, where ships would transport it around the world.

2. Quarrymen's houses and tunnel

Walk a short distance along the main Bangor road and turn left into David's Lane.

Head up towards the rows of terraced houses lying in the shadow of the mountain. In 1895 these were considered quality accommodation for the quarry workers and have stood the test of time.

Pass David Street and enter a tunnel taking you underneath the old quarry conveyor **(SH 716762)**.

Exit the tunnel and turn right into Gilfach Road and walk up the hill towards Craiglwyd Terrace – a pretty lane, with small quaint cottages and terraced houses.

Ahead of you, the road levels out, to reveal some great views down over the sea, east towards the Great Orme and west towards Anglesey and Puffin Island.

Looking across to Anglesey

Old farmhouse

Luscious green fields line the roadside here and you'll walk past an old, whitewashed farmhouse on your right.

Continue along the road for approximately 600 yards and turn right up a narrow lane towards the fisheries (marked with a footpath sign straight after the turning for Graiglwyd Hall). This is the start of the steeper section of the walk.

3. Graiglwyd Springs Fishery: SH 724757

Graiglwyd Springs is a former waterboard pumping station and now a popular haunt for local fishermen who come here for the prized trout.

Walk up the road and at the entrance to the fishery, turn right onto a public footpath skirting its southern edge. Follow the path around the perimeter, over a stile,

turn left and head up into the fields beyond.

4. Plas Uchaf farmhouse: SH 726757

Follow the track into a wide open field with Plas Uchaf farmhouse on your left. Continue on through the field, heading for the far left corner.

Fields above Plas Uchaf farmhouse

5. Kissing gate: SH 726759

Pass through the kissing gate and turn right onto Mountain Lane, which rapidly steepens.

Whilst you're huffing and puffing your way up the hill, keep an eye out for butterflies amongst the wild flowers that line the verges here in summer.

You'll soon walk under some shady oak trees and emerge at a cattle grid.

Keep going straight up the hill until you reach the Jubilee Pillars, where you'll find a picnic table so that you can sit down and enjoy the coastal views.

6. Jubilee Pillars: SH 731760

The pillars mark the start of the Jubilee Path around Foel Lus which opened to commemorate the 1887 Golden Jubilee of Queen Victoria.

This particular circular walk takes around three-quarters of an hour to complete and could be added to this route, if you're feeling fit!

Dry stone walling

If you look up to the top of Cerrig Gwynion in the distance (to the south-west) you'll notice some large standing stones which form part of a Druid stone circle.

5,000 years ago, stonemasons were quarrying here for stone for making hand axes for local use and for export. Many unfinished examples have been found nearby, suggesting they quarried and roughly shaped them on site but finished and polished them elsewhere.

Don't follow the Jubilee Path; instead turn right and follow a steep gravel track that hugs the edge of Foel Lus to your left.

7. Marker stone

Walk up the track towards a large white marker stone, giving directions for the Huw Tom Upland Walk, Druid stone circle and other routes.

At the next signpost, veer left and follow a grassy trail which splits into three.

Keep right, ignoring the signpost for Ty'n y Ffridd farm and stay on the middle track.

8. Stone wall and stile: SH 734753

Follow the bend around, passing a rocky crag until you spot a large stone boundary wall with a wooden stile and signpost for a public footpath.

Walk down towards the wall (which incidentally connects with another walking route further up) and cross over the stile.

9. Wooden footbridge: SH 738751

Turn left and make your way across a boggy area, passing large boulders on your way towards another stile and footbridge taking you over the River Gyrach.

The Victorians believed the stream here was named after a hideous witch who lived at the source of the river.

To your left now are fabulous views over the Great Orme and you might even catch a glimpse of the Gwynt y Môr windfarm situated off the coast near Llandudno.

The fields here were divided into long narrow strips during the Middle Ages and you can still see the old field boundaries when the bracken has died back.

The dry stone wall boundaries were built well over a hundred years ago. They not only keep livestock enclosed but also offer shelter to the animals and wildlife in this vast expanse of wilderness.

10. Waun Gyrach abandoned settlement: SH 740749

Make your way up the hill passing the romantic, abandoned settlement of Waun Gyrach which the local sheep now call home.

At the top of this grassy hill are even more amazing views with the wonderfully sculpted hills of Cerrig y Ddinas, which, if you half squint, resemble a sleeping dragon.

You'll soon become accustomed to hills on this walk as they continually roll on as you search for the elusive village of Rowen.

High up on the hillside of Cefn Maen Amor (to your right) is an impressive-looking boulder, probably deposited here after the last Ice Age. You might care to visit the boulder, if you're feeling fit, or ignore it and continue on, past the sheep-pens (**SH 744746**).

Here, all of the sheep belonging to different farmers were herded from the uplands into the main pen and then sorted into the smaller pens (petals), depending on who they belonged to.

On your left is the ruined farmstead of Tyddyn Grasod, a testament to the harsh conditions the smallholders endured here. But the views towards Conwy Castle, the Conwy valley and the mountains are fantastic.

This area is littered with Bronze Age burial cairns as well as Iron Age stone circles and standing stones, so it's well worth taking an OS map with you to pinpoint their exact locations.

Follow a grassy track to the right – keeping the pens on your left – and then continue along the dry stone wall, enjoying its shelter if the wind is up.

11. Stream crossing: SH 745736

Head down into the pass below and cross over a shallow stream. The trail leads you down into a dip and as you make your way up between two small hills, cross over the stone wall which is now on your right hand side.

As the ground levels out the track divides in two. Keep right and continue for some distance until you arrive at a spot where the wall has collapsed, opposite Caer Bach hillfort.

13. Caer Bach hillfort: SH 745730

This small Iron Age hillfort, situated on a rounded hill, dates from the first millennium BC and has commanding views over the Conwy valley and river below.

A little further on, you'll come to a small gated animal enclosure and beautifully crafted stone stile, built into the wall but easily overlooked as it blends in seamlessly. Pass through an iron gate and continue as far as an old stone gatepost.

14. Huw Tom's house: SH 740723

At the gatepost, turn left into the field and walk diagonally down towards a ruined cottage in the corner. This cottage, called Pen y Ffridd, was the childhood home of Huw Tom.

In 1906, aged 14, Huw walked to and from work at Graiglwyd Quarry every day, following a similar path to the one we're on.

From these humble beginnings Huw Tom became known as the 'Unofficial Prime Minister of Wales'.

As a boy, Huw Tom worked with his dad in the quarry but eventually ran away to south Wales to work in the coalmines.

After being wounded in the First World War, he returned to work in the granite quarries of north Wales where he became prominent in the trade union movement and in the Labour Party.

He later became an important, influential figure in Welsh public life from the period of the Attlee government, becoming the first chairman of the Council of Wales and Monmouthshire in 1949, and producing important reports on devolution.

Huw was a devout socialist and a member of the Labour Party throughout most of his life. He did join Plaid Cymru in 1959, but he reverted to his former allegiance in 1965.

He famously declined an invitation to be knighted at the time of the investiture of the Prince of Wales at Caernarfon Castle in July 1969. Not a bad career for a man with very little education from such a humble background.

15. Stone stile: SH 741722

Below you now is the village of Rowen, the River Conwy (marked as Afon Conwy on OS maps) and the Clwydian hills in the distance to the east.

Head through the wooden gate and walk diagonally across the field towards a stone wall with a stile built into it.

The stile can be difficult to spot but look for an old ivy bush growing over the wall and you'll soon find it.

The route from here can be tricky to follow as there are various alternative grassy tracks taking you down the hill, but bear right and head in a southerly direction towards the burial chamber and a wooded area in the distance.

As you near the trees, you'll pass over a normally dry river ditch which does fill up during rainy periods, so you may have to find an alternative crossing point higher up.

16. Maen y Bardd (the Bard's stone): SH 741719

This Neolithic burial chamber is situated below Pen y Ffridd and stands next to a Roman road which you will follow down into the village of Rowen.

Maen y Bardd burial chamber

The Roman road to Rowen

In the late afternoon, with the sunlight blasting down through a threatening sky, this spot can feel very magical.

You can understand why our ancestors chose this place to bury their dead, aligning them in a specific direction with the River Conwy below.

17. The Roman road to Rowen: SH 744719

The Roman road down to Rowen is a lovely way to end the walk, with commanding views all the way down to the village. You'll pass the local youth hostel as you walk down a very steep hill.

On rainy days this route can become very slippery with water cascading down off the hills and mountains, so wear proper footwear.

18. Entering Rowen village: SH 755720

Rowen village stands on an old drovers' route which once took cattle from Anglesey all the way to the markets in England.

These days Rowen is a quiet, picturesque village full of quirky old cottages, with the Afon Roe, a tributary of the River Conwy, flowing down behind the houses.

Follow the road down the hill and at the junction in the village, veer left and walk down past the Tŷ Gwyn pub.

19. End of the walk – Huw Tom memorial stone: SH 760720

A little further on, next to a small footbridge spanning the river, is a granite memorial stone commemorating Huw Tom's life. It reads 'Hewn from the rock, Welsh Patriot, Trade Unionist, Socialist, Author'.

A bus-stop, where you can catch a bus back to your car, is situated a little further down the road on the left hand side. Buses leave from Rowen to Conwy once every hour, where you can join more frequent bus and train services back to Penmaenmawr.

Derek says. . .

THERE ARE MORE sheep than people in Radnorshire, so if you want to get away from it all and enjoy some peace and quiet, then this walk is for you.

There's plenty to see, including a waterfall and breathtaking views, with the Cambrian Mountains to the west and the Wye Valley to the south.

Look out for Maen Serth, an impressive Bronze Age standing stone, on the top of Esgair Dderw. This marks the spot of an infamous murder in the 12th century, when two brothers were killed by a Norman Marcher Lord.

The highlight for me was the Gilfach Nature Reserve with its wonderful woodland, birds, lichen and leaping salmon. If you're very lucky, you may spot the rare watervole or even an otter. I did see a bird of prey but if you don't, there's always the Red Kite Centre just down the road, where it's pretty much guaranteed they will turn up at feeding time.

Rhayader holds the record for the lowest temperature in Wales, −23.3 Celsius in January 1940, but a warm welcome is guaranteed in one of the many watering holes. There are more pubs per head here than in any other town in the UK, so there's no chance of going thirsty after your walk!

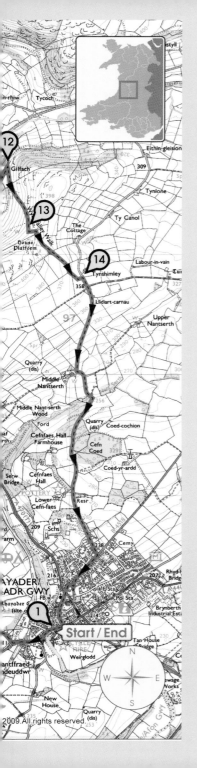

Rhayader

Approximate distance: 9 miles

Great Welsh Walks

Distance: 9 miles
Map: *OS Explorer Map: 200*
Introduction: *A stunning, strenuous 9 mile walk through quiet walking country with breathtaking views over the Wye Valley. From Rhayader you'll head off up into the hills along an old drovers' route, passing a Bronze Age standing stone before dropping down into a wide valley, arriving at the Gilfach Nature Reserve. Following the river, you'll walk part of the Monk's Trod trail as you head back to Rhayader taking in waterfalls, wildlife and a 15th century Welsh longhouse.*

1. Bridge over the River Wye: SN 969679

Starting on the bridge in the town, walk over the river – already 20 miles from its source near the summit of Pumlumon in the Cambrian Mountains – and head west out of town following the B4518.

Around the bend and a short distance down the road there's a turning to the left. It's not part of this walk but leads down to a tranquil spot by the river and worth a detour, if you have time.

Continue along the B4518 out of town, passing ornate wooden carvings marking the gateway to the Elan Valley Walking Trail.

Staying with the road, walk up the hill and follow the signpost for the Aberystwyth Mountain Road. Turn right, taking care when crossing the road, and continue for just over ½ mile, turning right onto another minor road **(SN 959684)**.

You'll soon arrive at a gate on your left hand side leading to Cwmdeuddwr Common, opposite a farm with a sign Llawr Dderw.

2. Cwmdeuddwr Common: SN 961686

Follow a rough 4x4 track up the hill past a house on your left and up the broad ridge beyond. This area is common land and was once the site of a golf course.

The walking track is the path on the left, with a 4x4 track over to your right. Head up a rocky track, steep in places with ferns and bracken on either side, until you reach the top of the ridge.

The views from up here are outstanding, with the Cambrian Mountains to the west and the Wye Valley to the south. Follow a winding grassy track up a gradual slope.

Along the way you'll spot the wind-farm over at Bryn Titli and the A470 winding around the River Wye below.

Briefly join the 4x4 track for a short stretch before turning back onto the grassy track and continue straight along a broad ridge. This was an old drovers' route used for taking cattle over the hills to the markets in England.

3. Maen Serth standing stone: SN 943699

On the top of Esgair Dderw is an impressive Bronze Age standing stone: 'maen' is Welsh for 'large stone', whilst 'serth' means 'steep'.

Standing at roughly seven feet high this stone would have served as a waymark for thousands of years to generations of travellers.

The stone also marks the spot of an infamous murder in the

Maen Serth standing stone

12th century when two brothers, Cadwallon and Einon Clud, were murdered by Roger Mortimer, a Norman Marcher Lord, after he was beaten by Einon in a jousting tournament.

Walk down the other side of the hill towards a rectangular shaped area of land, fenced off to prevent unauthorised off-road vehicles from churning up the ground.

4. Head down the valley: SN 939670

Veer right and pick up a rough indistinct track leading down

through the valley between the Moelfryn and Gamallt hills.

Gradually the track becomes steeper and more prominent as you make your way down through the heather and wild bilberries to a wider, stony track.

As you approach the valley basin, the views are jaw-dropping and, out of the wind, you can make out the sounds of babbling brooks and bleating sheep in the valley.

Head down through the ferns, passing shrubs and rowan trees clinging to the sides of the slopes before passing through a wooden gate with rocky crags, slate and heather up above.

Walk through a wooded area on your left and turn left down through a lovely oak forest but take care, as the track is uneven and very steep **(SN 944706)**. At the bottom, follow the fence line along a muddy track to a gate and turn left onto a quiet back road, with the River Wye opposite **(SN 945707)** and continue for about one mile.

At the fork in the road, turn right, following signs for Nannerth Fawr and walk up the lane.

5: Nannerth Fawr farm: SN 947715

This traditional 200 acre Welsh hill farm is a haven for birds and wildlife.

Walk up the road leaving the farm behind, passing some oak woods onto a road with nice views down the valley.

Heading towards Nannerth Fawr farm

Gilfach is a 410 acre hill farm and nature reserve, owned and managed by Radnorshire Wildlife Trust.

The reserve is home to around 1,300 species and is renowned for its broad-leaved woodland, birds, lichen and leaping salmon in the autumn.

Walk along the road to a wooden signpost and head down a grassy track, following the signs for Nature Trail and Monk's Trod **(SN 957715)**.

6. Wooden bench: SN 948721

Just beyond a wooden bench, turn right and follow a grassy track down through the trees.

This track runs parallel to the road you've just walked along and the river below. The route brings you out into a wide field with a large stone on one side.

Walk across the field and through a gap between some smaller stones into the next field. Follow the path leading down along the fence line towards a wooden gate. Walk through, entering a light woodland with glimpses of the river to your left.

Cistercian monks used to ride on horseback along here, using specially devised routes linking up the nearby abbeys of Strata Florida and Cwm Hir which were 25 miles apart, the distance most monks could travel on horseback in a day.

To the right is a small pond which was recently created to attract water voles. Apparently, it's been remarkably successful but you're unlikely to spot one unless you're very quiet and extremely lucky!

Continue on past an old winching post, a remnant of the railway, and walk past the old railway tunnel.

7. Pont Marteg: SN 951716

You'll soon arrive at a narrow wooden footbridge with views up and down the river. This area is popular with kayakers who launch from just below the bridge. Cross over and walk up a slight incline, arriving at a layby alongside the A470.

Take care crossing over this busy road and follow a tarmac road towards the Gilfach Nature Reserve, where you will find a couple of parking areas.

9. Railway tunnel: SN 959714

The Mid Wales Railway opened in 1864 and was a vital route for coal during the First World War, linking up the south Wales coalfield with mid and north Wales.

The line ran from Three Cocks Junction in Aberllyfni to Llanidloes but was never financially viable. It closed in 1962.

8. Gilfach Nature Reserve: SN 952715

Set in the picturesque Marteg valley,

The railway line now provides an excellent habitat for wildlife,

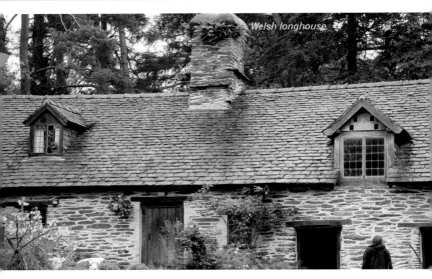

Welsh longhouse

particularly glowworms that relish the chippings, and owls and bats that live inside the tunnel.

Pass through the wooden gate and walk up through a small wooded area and out into a sheltered clearing, which is a favoured spot for butterflies in summer. Continue along a muddy track with views over the Gamallt hillside.

Turn left and cross over a small footbridge and through a wooden gate. Head along a grassy track above the river, passing rowan trees en route and follow a sloping track down to the river **(SN 960714)** where the curiously named bloody-nosed beetle is known to hang out.

At the bottom of the track, turn left through a gate and walk along the river. In addition to some scenic views, you may spot the occasional dipper bobbing its tail.

10. Sheep dip: SN 961713

Walk along a grassy area towards a deep pool next to a small waterfall, where you will see some remarkable rock formations carved out by the river. In the days before industrial

chemicals were introduced, local farmers used this spot to wash their sheep in the River Marteg.

Keep walking along the track, passing through a gate and the next field and then under a giant oak tree. Then on through another gate towards another clearing, until you reach an impressive waterfall to the right of the field.

11. Waterfall: SN 963715

There's a viewing platform here and in the autumn it's possible to see salmon leaping and even the occasional otter fishing.

Continue to the next gate and cross the field, passing an information board. After arriving at a railway bridge **(SN 962718)**, turn right and walk past a large wooden otter hide, following a tarmac road up a steep hill towards the visitor centre.

12. Radnorshire Wildlife Trust visitor centre: SN 965717

At the top of a winding road you'll arrive at the old farmyard within which stands a visitor centre and a stunning 15th century Welsh longhouse, fully restored by the wildlife trust's volunteers.

A farm was first built here in medieval times and it was added to in each century. It still contains many original features and a small exhibition gives a unique insight into how farmers once worked these lands.

To the right of the visitor centre is a track with wooden railings. Follow this and walk up the track above and behind the longhouse towards the hills **(SN 965716)**.

The large gate at the end of the track marks the edge of the reserve and you will now follow the Wye Valley Walk up the hill in a southerly direction for ⅓ mile **(SN 965715)**.

13. Views over the valley: SN 967713

On your way up the east side of Gamallt you'll be rewarded with some of the nicest views of the valley, looking down between Gamallt and Cefnbychan towards the Wye Valley, where you can often spot birds of prey soaring in the thermals above.

You'll also get a great view of the road which you walked up earlier, winding up through the nature reserve.

At the top, walk down to a metal gate and cross a wooden stile **(SN 967712)**.

The walk back is now fairly straightforward as you follow the fence line for ⅓ mile through farm fields back towards Rhayader **(SN 967712)**.

The views are still lovely though, as you look out over the hills to the east where the Monk's Trod route winds its way towards Abbey Cwm Hir.

Pass a small copse of pine trees on your right **(SN 968710)** and continue along the field boundary until you reach a wooden signpost for Gilfach Nature Reserve and Rhayader, which is 2 miles away.

14. The road back to Rhayader: SN 971708

Turn right and follow a winding, quiet back road, mostly downhill, back into town.

Derek says. . .

THIS ENERGETIC WALK is suitable for beginners and walkers of all ages. Skirrid Fawr is just 486 metres (1,595 feet) above sea level but feels like a proper mountain.

It's a steep climb to the top but you are rewarded with wonderful views of Abergavenny, the Blorenge and the Sugar Loaf, and on clear days as far as the Malvern Hills and the Bristol Channel.

The unusual shape of Skirrid Fawr, also known as the Holy Mountain, has led to many legends and superstitions. According to one, the missing chunk on its west side was caused by Noah's Ark! Another reckons it was caused by a bolt of lightning marking Christ's crucifixion.

Its distinct shape is actually the result of a landslip that occurred at the end of the last Ice Age. Near the summit are the remains of a medieval chapel, which give a spiritual feel to the place. It's also a great spot for a picnic but very exposed, so bring warm clothes.

At the end of the walk in Llanvihangel Crucorney, you can quench your thirst at the Skirrid Inn. It is reputed to be the oldest pub in Wales and the most haunted. If you're not easily spooked, it's a great place to stop off, especially on a cold winter's day when they've got a real fire going.

17. Skirrid

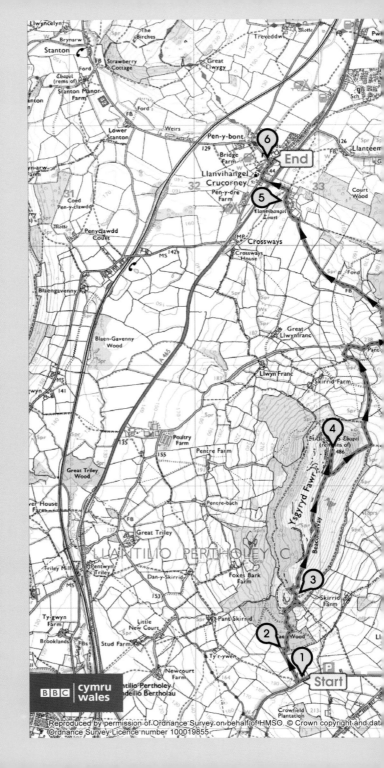

Skirrid

Approximate distance: 4 miles

Great Welsh Walks

Distance: 4 miles
Map: *OS Explorer Map: OL13*
Introduction: *A short, exhilarating walk up Skirrid Fawr and down to the Skirrid Inn in Llanvihangel Crucorney. The walk begins with a fairly steep climb to the summit, followed by a smooth downhill section and then mostly flat terrain across pretty countryside. The route follows part of the Beacon's Way, taking in Skirrid Fawr, Llanvihangel Court and the haunted Skirrid Inn.*
We did this as a linear walk but you can return along the paths below the Skirrid. Or you can take a bus back to Abergavenny, but it's still a walk or taxi ride back to your starting point.

1. Start of the walk: SO 329164

The walk begins in a lay-by just off the Old Ross Road (B4521), opposite Caer Wood.

Head through the first gate, down a gravel track, around a bend and then follow a path uphill to a wooden gate. Cross over the stile and follow the track past an information board and ornately carved oak bench.

2. Oak bench: SO 327166

The bench was carved by Welsh sculptor, Robert Jakes, from Welsh oak to mark the start of the Beacons Way and depicts the skyline of Skirrid Fawr, even showing the landslip as a notch in the wood.

From here the track soon gets steeper as you negotiate wooden steps up through the semi-natural

deciduous woodland, passing forestry tracks on both sides.

The National Trust has taken over the management of the forest from the Forestry Commission and has returned much of it back to native woodland, so you'll hear plenty of birds along the way.

The paths are well-maintained with wooden steps, drainage gullies and gravel but are best avoided during or immediately after heavy rain.

Keep to the main path and head up a steep track and steps past a wooden bench, handy for anyone wanting to catch their breath.

At the crossroads, head straight over and up the hill following a steep, winding woodland path up as far as an old wall and wooden gate.

Turn right and continue up the hill past a mossy wall on your right. At the fork in the trail beneath a large tree, keep left. To the right is the trail from the other side of the mountain.

3. Viewpoint: SO 328170

Walk up steep steps and down into a dip on the other side, past a wonderful moss-covered tree, to a viewpoint looking down over Monmouthshire and the Severn estuary.

Follow the path around a bend to a left hand turn and another viewpoint, giving you a sneak peek of the Black Mountains. Above you, to your right, is an area of exposed red sandstone.

Return to the main path and after a short walk you'll arrive at another viewpoint, with even better views over north Monmouthshire. Herefordshire is to your left and the Bristol Channel is down to the right.

Behind you is the Sugar Loaf, with the summit of Pen y Fan, the highest peak in southern Britain, in the far distance.

It's now a short stroll up to the southern end of the Skirrid. Walk along the spine of the mountain towards the highest point.

The name Skirrid/Ysgyryd Fawr is also known as the Holy Mountain. The Welsh word 'ysgyryd' means 'rugged' or 'rocky' – a reference perhaps to the craggy landslide on the western side of the ridge.

At the summit you'll find a trig point and two large boulders marking the entrance to an ancient chapel.

4. St Michael's Chapel: SO 331183

All that remains of the chapel that once stood here are the stones marking the entranceway and a depression in the earth. Possibly founded in the 10th century, the chapel was dedicated to St Michael and is surrounded by a circular earthwork.

It was in use until around 1680 and was a place of pilgrimage for centuries, particularly during times of religious persecution.

Local farmers would gather the red soil from around the mountain to spread on their land to ensure a good harvest.

The views are staggering: Herefordshire to the north; the Usk valley and Somerset to the south; Gloucester to the east and the Black Mountains and Brecon Beacons to the west.

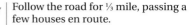

Retrace your steps for approximately 200m and turn left **(SO 331187)** onto a grassy track leading down the eastern edge of the mountain to sheep pastures below.

Keep straight on and follow signs for the Beacons Way trail, passing through a wooden gate on the far side **(SO 334184)**.

Walk down through the field to a stile beneath a large ash tree and cross over into the next field edged with hazel and oak trees.

Continue down the left hand side of the field and hop over a stile into the next field **(SO 334188)**.

Head towards the left hand corner, hop over another stile **(SO 333191)** and walk across the field towards its entrance near some farm buildings **(SO 332191)**.

Head through a gate and down through the next large sheep field, with views of the Sugar Loaf on your left.

Walk down to a metal gate standing next to a tree, cross over a stile and turn right onto a quiet country road.

Follow the road for ⅓ mile, passing a few houses en route.

Near a house called The Gables, turn left, following the signpost for 'Crucorney 2km', and walk towards large farm barns in the distance **(SO 337192)**.

Walk down through a long narrow field and into the next. Keep right along the woods and at the far end, under some trees, is a wooden footbridge.

Cross over into an overgrown, marshy field and, halfway across, veer left. Head through a metal gate at the edge of the trees **(SO 334196)**.

Enter a quiet woodland, walk across a footbridge and through a small metal gate next to an old stone marker **(SO 333197)**.

Walk across a large open field passing one lone tree and into the next field, which was full of hay bales during our walk in September **(SO 330198)**.

Aim towards the corrugated iron barns up ahead, keeping the fence line on your right **(SO 329201)**.

Walk past the first barn, through a wooden gate and turn left along a muddy track **(SO 328202)** that heads along the back of the farm towards Llanvihangel Court, a Tudor manor house dating from the 15th century.

5. Llanvihangel Court: SO 327203

The track runs past a large timber barn which would have once been used for corn storage. The barn wouldn't look out of place in the National History Museum at St Fagans.

Next door to the barn is the privately owned Tudor manor house, which has been described as 'the most richly decorated house of the early 1600s in Wales'. It contains examples of 17th century panelling, plaster

Old barn at Llanvihangel Court

ceilings and a magnificent oak staircase.

The house was reputedly used as a hideaway by King Charles I during the Civil War. It is open to the public from May to August at certain times and guided tours can be arranged.

Follow the track down the hill, past the manor house.

For a front view of the manor house, turn right through a wooden gate, following a rough vehicle track past some fir trees before emerging at a metal gate and two public footpaths.

Return to the main driveway and head towards the A465. Carefully cross the busy road and follow the lane opposite up into the village of Llanvihangel Crucorney **(SO 325206)**.

At the end of the lane, turn right and walk past St Michael's Church on the other side of the road. Follow the pavement down towards the petrol station and just beyond it, on the left, is the Skirrid Inn.

6. The Skirrid Inn: SO 326207

It's claimed that a pub has been here in some form or another since the 11th century, making it one of the oldest pubs in Wales. Most of what remains today dates from the 15th century.

Outside the pub is a mounting block for horses where Owain Glyndŵr is said to have stood and rallied his soldiers before attacking nearby villages and settlements sympathetic to Henry IV.

The first floor of the inn was used as a courtroom where sentences were handed out and executions took place: 185 convicted criminals were allegedly hanged here from a wooden beam above the staircase, which eerily has notches worn into it by the rope.

The pub is infamous for its paranormal activity and has been featured in a number of TV programmes about ghosts. A quick read of the visitor book is highly recommended to find out which rooms are haunted, if you're planning to stay the night!

This is where the walk ends. You could either catch a taxi from the pub straight back to your car, or hop on a bus to Abergavenny and take a taxi from there.

Derek says. . .

PEMBROKESHIRE is one of my favourite parts of Wales and is a walker's paradise. This long walk from Trefin to Pwll Deri is on a quieter section of the 186 mile coastal path.

You will pass hidden coves and a wonderful selection of beaches such as Abermawr. The scenery is amazing too: wild and dramatic, with towering cliffs and superb views.

Have your photograph taken next to Carreg Samson. This 5,000 year old cromlech or burial chamber gets its name from a local legend that Samson placed the capstone in position with his little finger!

Nearby is the picturesque village of Abercastle which has lots of history and a lovely harbour.

It's also worth having a look around Tregwynt woollen mill. It is open seven days a week and has a café where you can enjoy homemade treats like bara brith.

At the end of the walk, you could catch a bus back to Trefin from Trefasser near Fishguard, or why not stay over at the youth hostel in Pwll Deri? It has to be one of the best locations for a hostel in Wales, if not the whole of the UK. It's also a great spot for bird and seal watching.

Approximate distance: 10½ miles

Reproduced by permission of Ordnance Survey on behalf of HMSO. © Crown copyright and database right 2009 A

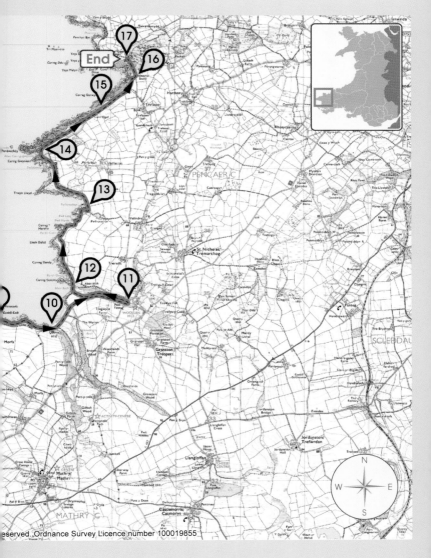

Distance: 10½ miles

Map: *OS Explorer Map OL35*

Introduction: *This epic 10½ mile trek along the Wales Coast Path begins in the coastal village of Trefin, situated half way between St Davids and Fishguard. Finding your way is easy as you are on the coastal path pretty much the whole time. Along the way you'll pass a 5,000-year old Neolithic burial chamber before dropping down into the picturesque fishing harbour at Abercastle. Dramatic clifftop paths take you along the coast to the finish at Pwll Deri hostel.*

1. Start of the walk – The Ship Inn, Trefin: SM 838325

From the Ship Inn, head west down Ffordd y Felin towards the coast, passing brightly painted cottages as you go.

As you leave the village and head down the hill, turn right off the main road and follow signposts towards the coast path.

The track here, which can get a little boggy, leads to an old ruined mill.

2. Trefin Mill: SM 834324

There isn't much left of the mill these days, which is situated above a pretty little cove. The small stream trickling seawards once powered a large mill wheel.

The Archdruid Crwys's most famous poem, 'Melin Trefin' features the historic mill here at Aberfelin.

Less than a hundred years ago, this mill was a hive of activity with boats sailing to and fro with wheat, ready to be milled into flour.

Leaving the mill, follow the path left, over a wooden footbridge and up a steep muddy track. On the hillside opposite, sat in a farmer's field, you'll see a modern stone circle erected for a past Eisteddfod.

3. Ruined house: SM 833328

After a while the track levels out and you'll arrive at another hill with loose shale underfoot. Pass through a wooden gate and head towards a ruined house on the top of the headland.

Abercastle harbour at low tide

From up here you'll begin to get a taster of the views and terrain that lie ahead in this very special part of the Pembrokeshire Coast National Park.

Keep right and continue up the hill, passing fields. Down below and to your left is Pwll Olfa, a pristine cove with some of the most translucent, blue water you'll ever encounter.

Continue along the path, enjoying the coastline as well as the vibrant coastal plants scattered in amongst the gorse banks and dry stone walls. Passing Pwll Llong, head up a steep section of the trail towards a signpost for Longhouse Farm.

4. Longhouse Farm: SM 843334

This farm, once a hotspot for daffodil production in the area, is now managed by the National Trust. Head down into a sheltered grassy valley complete with badger setts, so watch where you're treading.

Head up to a wooden gate and admire the stunning views below with sculpted sea caves on the left hand side of the bay.

Pass through the gate and follow the bay around to Castell Coch, one of two forts en route and a great place to have a bite to eat and escape the wind. Take care along this section, as the high cliffs are very steep.

The clifftops provide excellent views of the coast to the south-west, with Penbiri and Carn Llidi in the distance. On clear days you can make out the white marker stones at the entrance to Porthgain harbour.

The path steers you well away from danger but the temptation is always there to take a closer look at the coves below. But keep well away, as you can never be sure how safe the cliff edges are.

Sea-arch

5. Views across to a sea-arch: SM 841339

Just north of here, you'll cross over into farmland and to your left is a wonderful example of a natural sea-arch.

Keep heading east across fields towards Abercastle with Ynys Deullyn to the north.

As you head down a grassy track towards Abercastle you'll spot signposts for Carreg Samson, an impressive burial chamber and a must see on this walk as it's only a short detour off the coastal path.

6. Carreg Samson: SM 848335

This 5,000-year-old burial chamber or cromlech stands in splendid isolation overlooking the bay above Abercastle.

The large capstone, measuring 15 feet by 9 feet, rests on three of the seven upright stones. The structure was once covered by a mound of earth.

Carreg Samson

Legend tells of how St Samson once lifted the 15 foot long capstone into place using just one finger!

Whatever you believe, this site was of great significance to the ancient people who gathered here to bury their dead.

Walk back to the path and turn right towards Abercastle. Head down the steps, taking care – as some of the rocks are slippery – and follow the trail along to the harbour.

Keep an eye out for old cannons which have been placed along the route before you pass an old limekiln.

7. Abercastle: SM 853336

Abercastle is a former trading harbour which once exported slate, grain, lime, butter, honey and corn. These days, the harbour is mainly used by local fishermen and leisure craft.

In 1876, it was also the landing site of the first single-handed Atlantic sailing west to east by Alfred 'Centennial' Johnson, a Danish-born fisherman.

It took Alfred an incredible 66 days to complete his journey and you'll find a commemorative plaque by the slipway.

Head towards the opposite side of the harbour, following a track past a stream and head up the steps (SM 853337).

Walk up behind the cottages and continue along the coastal path. The views along this stretch are some of the prettiest you'll encounter on this walk as you look back towards Abercastle and the small island of Ynys y Castell guarding the harbour entrance.

Ahead of you are numerous small islands and rocky crags, Pembrokeshire's version of tropical atolls, surrounded by a turquoise sea. The track takes you past more pristine coves, and wild flowers and heather abound.

8. Pwllstrodur: SM 867337

A steep track leads you down to Pwllstrodur but you'll soon realise that what goes down must go back up, so prepare yourself for a steep climb up the other side of the hillside.

This dark, pebble-strewn cove, best visited at low tide, is a popular haunt of local naturists, so be

Abercastle

Coastline near Abermawr

prepared to see some naked flesh if you venture here in late summer.

Cross over a small wooden footbridge and climb up the steep hillside onto the next headland.

Passing Aber Mochyn, another cove with black sand, and Porth Glastwr, you'll arrive at your second hillfort for today, also confusingly called Castell Coch. This one overlooks the pebbled beaches of Abermawr and Aberbach.

9. Castell Coch promontory fort: SM 872347

The fort is difficult to see in summer when it's engulfed by greenery but as you walk past, you should be able to see signs of a defensive, double embankment. The fort had an unusual zigzagging pathway leading to its heart, making it difficult to attack.

10. Abermawr: SM 881344

Follow your nose along the coast and down to the pebble beach at Abermawr via a steep and narrow track.

As you make your way down, keep an eye out for an old storage tunnel under the steps, left over from the area's quarrying days.

The famous engineer, Isambard Kingdom Brunel, once proposed this sheltered bay as the main harbour and railway terminus for transport to Ireland but thankfully his plans were abandoned and Neyland was chosen instead.

This beach was also home to a cable station and in 1862, the cable ship, *Bewick* laid 60 miles of cable from Abermawr to Wexford. A second cable was laid in 1880 from Abermawr to Blackwater in Ireland.

12. Aberbach: SM 884350

From the mill, walk back towards Abermawr but before reaching the end of the road, turn right onto a track heading through fields in order to rejoin the coastal path down to Aberbach.

Local folklore says that a farmer once caught a mermaid here and kept her in his house, which was cursed until she was released.

11. Melin Tregwynt Mill: SM 894349

If you'd like to visit the woollen mill, take the pathway to your right, leading up to the road and follow it as far as the mill, where you'll find a café and toilets.

The whitewashed woollen mill has stood on this site since the 17th century. Originally, local farmers used to bring their fleeces to be spun into yarn and woven into fine woollen blankets. Nowadays, the mill supplies top end luxury goods to shops all over the world and is open to the public.

At the far end of this pebbly bay is a stream trickling down into the sea. Pass this and turn left up a relatively steep, winding track to more level ground, where you'll pass over another stream.

From up here you'll get a nice view back over the two beaches you've just walked across. Stay on the coastal path now, enjoying the cliff and sea views as you go.

If you're walking this section in the autumn, keep an eye out for grey seal pups in the coves below and porpoises feeding out to sea.

back to Aberbach via Velindre, if you prefer a shorter walk.

Stay away from the cliff edge, and keep inside the stone wall that has been placed there for your safety.

Pass through a wooden gate and follow a stony track down into a sheltered valley, full of ferns and golden flowering gorse in summer.

Cross over the wooden footbridge at the bottom and make your way up a steep and winding muddy track. Trek along the clifftops passing Pwlldawnau, Aber Cerrig Gwynion and Penbwchdy points.

14. Round stone shelter: SM 879373

Near the headland at Penbwchdy you'll arrive at a circular, roofless, dry stone enclosure, which once housed livestock but now provides a great wind shelter and spot to have a rest.

Keep going, following a track up and over a steep rocky ridge and continue along the rocky track down the other side.

15. Coastal views: SM 885377

From up here you'll get some of the best views along this walk, with Garn Fawr to the north-east and a sprinkling of tiny islands and rocky outcrops below.

13. Pwllcrochan: SM 886363

Follow a winding path down to the jagged sea cliffs at Pwllcrochan. Take care along this section, as parts of the path are close to the cliff edge. The path is steep and uneven, so keep dogs (and children!) on a tight leash.

Access to the small beach below is not advisable.

Head over a wooden stile, down the steps and up into a sheltered, fern-filled valley with a stream running down one side.

At the top, turn left. Turning right would take you on a circular route

You can also finally see the finishing point – a large, whitewashed house, now a youth hostel, balanced precariously above the cliffs at Pwlll Deri.

Follow the path for another mile and turn right, up a narrow grassy track leading to a minor road.

It's a quiet road but cars do use it to access the hostel and a scattering of local houses nearby, so take care.

16. Dewi Emrys memorial stone: SM 893387

Turn left onto the road and after a short distance you'll arrive at a memorial stone for the poet Dewi Emrys (1879–1952), whose poem, 'Pwll Deri', celebrates the area's character and wildlife.

Dewi won the Chair at the National Eisteddfod on four occasions but infamously pawned his 1926 Eisteddfod Crown in Swansea.

17. End of the walk – Pwll Deri Hostel: SM 892387

Follow the main road towards the hostel perched on an idyllic clifftop setting, with spectacular views and glorious sunsets.

It's a great place for bird and seal watching too and a wonderful spot to base yourself for walks along the coast path.

Turn left down the driveway and you'll see the hostel ahead. The impressive Garn Fawr hillfort, situated on the highest point of the Pen Caer/Strumble Head peninsula, overlooks the hostel.

Time your walk right and you can catch the Strumble Shuttle bus service back to the start.

The shuttle bus runs from Fishguard to St Davids, seven days a week during the summer and the nearest bus stop to Pwll Deri is at Trefasser Cross (around ½ mile away), which will take you back to Trefin.

During the winter months, there is a reduced service, so you might want to hop in a taxi to Goodwick instead (4 miles away) and catch a bus back from there.

Also available:
the two original *Weatherman Walking* books

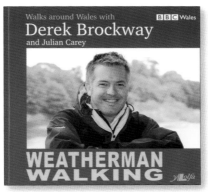

A fully illustrated guide to twelve walks, grouped around the seasons. They are mainly in south, west and mid Wales. As well as detailed directions, the guide gives an insight into the heritage, social history, wildlife and topography of the areas described.
ISBN: 978-0-86243-917-0
£7.95

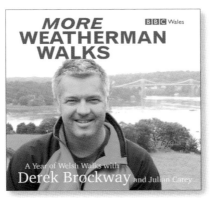

A second selection of twelve walks based on Derek Brockway's television travels; includes maps, directions and an insight into the social history, heritage, wildlife and topography of some of Wales's most attractive landscapes.
ISBN: 978-1-84771-058-1
£9.95

We publish a wide range of Welsh-interest books. For a full list simply browse our website, where you may search and order online. If you prefer a paper catalogue, please contact us directly. Support your local bookshop if you can.

Talybont, Ceredigion, Wales SY24 5HE
website www.ylolfa.com
e-mail ylolfa@ylolfa.com
tel. 01970 832 394
fax 01970 832 782